# HARRISON CONNECTIONS

Tom Harrison's
'Desire to communicate'

~

to prove what he always
said was true.

Collated and written
by

# Ann Harrison

Published by
Saturday Night Press Publications
England.
www.snppbooks.com
*snppbooks@gmail.com*

ISBN 978-1-908421-11-1

Printed by Lightning Source
www.lightningsource.com

www.snppbooks.com

Cover design by Ann Harrison - Saturday Night Press Publications
Photo © Ann Harrison - 'Tom Harrison doing what he loved best.'

The colours yellow and blue are those of the International Code of
Signals flag for 'Desire to communicate' see p.210-11.

## *Dedication*

to all our friends and companions in both worlds,
who have assisted us in bringing this book
into being, in the hope of helping those who
read it to realize what is possible
when there is abiding love.

# Acknowledgements

*My profound thanks go to all those friends who are mediums, and friends who say they are not, for giving Tom the opportunity to connect, and for passing on the connections with Tom throughout these four years.*

*He has been able to connect through you, and with you, in so many different ways which gave me support through my loss but more importantly has enabled me to give to the world the truth he so propounded.*

*~ There is no separation and we can connect across the veil of 'Death'.*

*My thanks go also to:*

*~ Sue Farrow, Editor of 'Psychic News' for permission to include her tribute to Tom and 'All tied up' both previously published on the internet site – Spirit of PN, and to Roy Stemman who first released Sue's tribute on his site ParanormalReview.com;*

*~ Katie Halliwell for permission to include the piece she wrote for her book 'Experiences of Trance, Physical Mediumship and Associated Phenomena with the Stewart Alexander Circle'(Pt3);*

*~ Dr Anabela Cardoso for permission to reprint the article 'Sou o Tom', from ITC Journal No 41;*

*~ Dr Annette Childs for permission to quote from her article 'Got Grief' and Tom and Lisa Butler in whose AA-EVP Journal (Winter 2011) it was first printed;*

*~ Marjorie Hesford for permission to include a passage from the book 'Facts' rec'd. by A. Borgia (Two Worlds Publishing Co.);*

*~ Robert McLernon and Diane Milner for checking and advising on the text.*

# Contents

# Foreword

Throughout life's journey, we may, if we are fortunate enough, meet with a fellow traveller who is destined to impact upon our lives in a most unique and singular way. It may be that he or she shares our understanding of and/or philosophy in respect of matters which we hold close to our heart. It may be that their personality and/or their intense interests match those of our own. There can be many reasons for such an immediate connection but to try and quantify and qualify such an attraction will ofttimes meet only with failure. We can only say that such events do occur – that such individuals can enter and touch our lives in a most wonderful positive and occasionally, in a dramatic enriching way.

During the spring of 1989, I purchased a booklet entitled; *Visits by Our Friends from the Other Side*, which was a séance room chronicle of a materialisation medium from the 1950s called Minnie Harrison. Written by her son Tom Harrison, from diary entries and recorded notes that he had meticulously made at the time, it described in some detail the extraordinary events that he had personally witnessed within his parents' own séance room. But, as I began to read it, I could not possibly have imagined that soon its author would enter into, and impact upon, my own life in a quite wonderful way. Looking back now I can see clearly that he was the kind of person that I wrote of in my first paragraph. A rare individual who truly touched and enriched my own life.

Whilst the booklet introduced me to a physical medium of whom I had previously had no knowledge, it also resulted in my wish to learn more, and so, after reading its final page, I wrote to its author with a series of questions. Shortly afterwards I received a reply, in which Mr Harrison (as he then was to me) wrote 'I was delighted to know that you enjoyed the book, but, as I said, it did not even scratch the surface of the eight years of remarkable and, as you say, tangible phenomena every Saturday evening.' And so began our frequent correspondence which culminated in our eventual meeting the following year.

When it occurred, it was not like two people meeting for the first time as strangers – not at all. Rather, it was two people meeting as friends – relaxed and delighted to be in each other's company. In the years that followed that did not change and often I was to witness how, when meeting strangers, his very persona instantly created a relaxed atmosphere.

Tom was a remarkable man, who gladly shared his knowledge and conviction regarding survival and communication with anyone interested in this most vital of questions with which man has wrestled since he first set foot upon this earth; 'Do we survive the grave'? Tom knew that we did, and delivered a countless number of talks over many years around the world, concerning his many past dramatic séance room experiences. Indeed, on a great many occasions he spoke at my own residential seminars and never failed to engross and fascinate his audience. His sincerity on such occasions spoke volumes. Never would there be any doubt that here was a man who spoke directly from the heart, and to be in his presence, was to be in the presence of a friend. It was my pleasure – it was my delight – it was my own privilege to have known him.

And finally – what follows is Ann Harrison's personal and sincere account and record of his after-death efforts to communicate with her and with his many friends. There can be no doubt that he is intent on continuing his lifelong work from his new perspective.

Stewart Alexander
February 6th, 2015

# Preface

Tom always ended his talks about the phenomena and contact experienced in their home circle with his mother as the medium, by saying:

> What you have seen and heard today is not proof to you as individuals. It was proof to me, but for you it is only evidence, which is commensurate with the credibility of the source, as in a court of Law.
>
> I trust I have impressed you as an honest and genuine witness with sincerity and integrity. I have no reason to be otherwise. There is no personal motive at any time.

This applies also to what I have written. It is not proof to you, but I give you it as evidence and it depends on the credibility you place in me, as to whether you believe it or not.

I have no financial interest in writing this book. All profits go to our support of those with cancer. My only aim is to tell you what has happened through the efforts of this wonderful man, who spent the best part of his earthly life telling all who would listen of the contact he had with family and friends who had passed over. To know that their support and love continues from the world beyond.

In the late1940s, Tom spoke to Jack Graham about what he witnessed in the circle. Jack had a 'rival' fish and chip shop, a few streets away from Tom and his Mam. As Tom helped him prepare the fish for the lunch-time opening they chatted.

Jack expressed an interest and an opportunity arose for him to be at the circle one Saturday evening, and there met his 'dead' family. Jack passed very suddenly, just one week after that visit to the circle. He had, as a young man, been one of the Plymouth Brethren, and through his visit to the circle was helped to understand there was more to life than just our physical existence. He soon returned from the spirit world to let them know he had made it through.

On one occasion, years later, when Tom should have been overseeing the Mess Games for the evening, he was 'persuaded' to show his photos of the materialised spirit people to the inspecting General at the Army Reserve annual training camp. He discovered that the General knew about such phenomena, as his grandmother had been a medium. In those days Tom always had the photos with him. He was enthusiastic and unstoppable.

He has continued to strive hard since his 'death' in October 2010, to show that what he said was true – that you can connect across the veil of death. He has communicated in almost all the different ways we know of, to show he is so close. As he said recently, the gap between the worlds is much smaller than we think.

Our family and friends, our guides and companions are near us, so close; not to interfere with our lives, but to give us strength and comfort when we need it, if we will only acknowledge their presence.

What I have written may seem far-fetched to many of you. Twenty-four years ago, I knew nothing of happenings like these before my first husband returned, just three weeks after his death in 1990, to tell us he was fine. So I can only say to you it happened and continues to do so.

Tom instructed me to write this book through telepathy and through several mediums – even giving one of them the title of the book.

I do so hope that this account of part of the last four years of my life may help you in your search and understanding. This has been a journey through grief and loss, until now, I feel I am standing on my own two feet again. Ready to make a difference. If you don't understand some of the terms I use please look at the glossary at the end of the book – 'What do we mean by...' or contact me through my website.

If you are grieving take heart, and seek out someone to help, if you feel you cannot make contact yourself. Look for those who are sent to you by others, for they will have been chosen by your family for the support they can give.

If you are searching for knowledge and understanding, keep going. Open your heart and mind. Expect nothing, desire nothing, but allow them to draw close and guide you, in whatever way your family, and those advanced ones, whom we call guides, are able to reach you, so that you too may help others. For only in this way may the glorious light of loving kindness spread throughout our world.

God bless you all.

Ann Harrison
Eagles Nest
October 23rd, 2014.

*One*

# Love changes everything

Many of you may never have heard the name – Tom Harrison nor that of his mother, Minnie Harrison.

Twenty years ago I hadn't when a friend persuaded me to go for a weekend break at *Fir Trees Spiritual Centre*, near Howden, only twenty miles away. There, besides a Harvest Psychic Supper, Tom Harrison was to speak about his mother's amazing mediumship in their home circle in the 1940s/50s. They had had every conceivable type of physical phenomena from apports and writings to trumpet voices and full, solid materializations in red light.

I had been told that nobody 'did' physical mediumship anymore. It was the 'lowest of energies' they said at the Spiritualist Church I attended. "We need the higher teachings which can only come from Spirit through the mind," they said.

"But it helps raise funds for the centre if we go and stay!" was my friend's answer. An overnight stay at that centre was like a fortnight's holiday, such was the welcome – and the peace.

The decision to attend was to change my life. Tom and I were instantly attracted, even before we spoke. A connection that reached beyond time was rekindled and the inevitable happened.

Within a few weeks, invitations for him to give his talk came pouring in. I offered to do the driving all over the North of England and Scotland so that he could tell people about the amazing phenomena he had witnessed in their home circle. A meeting with Professor Archie Roy at Stansted Hall led to the *Scottish Society for Psychical Research* flying him to Glasgow so they could hear about the phenomena.

Tom was passionate about telling everyone what he had witnessed and passing on the knowledge that 'There is no death'. He didn't just believe it; he KNEW it. He had spoken with over 1500 materialised people in the ten years they had the circle before his mother's death in 1958. All were known and, in the red light they used, recognised by the circle members, or known to someone visiting the circle on that occasion.

The following spring he started on the filming of a video of his talk through a 'connection' made when Tom stayed with Pat and Tony Hamblin, near Wakefield in June 1993. He had not met them before, but they were soon enjoying each others' company. During the morning following his talk, he learned that part of Pat's work at the Wakefield College of Further education was to make training videos. Tom told them of his daughter Joyce's 'wild' idea. She had suggested that he make a video of his talk – because as she had said "You are not getting any younger, and you won't be around for ever." Pat jumped at the idea and offered her husband, Tony (with a PhD. in Organic Chemistry) as the cameraman. Throughout that summer, they went with Tom to film his talks and interview the last few people who had also been to the circle.

Tom even had a post-production expert in the line-up – a man he had met when filming with Alan Pemberton for the video *Science of Eternity*. However, as so often happens, when the films were ready to be edited, the 'expert' on the South Coast, couldn't do the work. Fortunately, our local *Yellow*

*Pages* came to the rescue. Only two miles down the road from my home there was a sympathetic post-production man with his own business. And his wife just happened to be a medium whom we had already met when we had organised a Natural Healing Exhibition in the local town a few months earlier! We had hit the Jackpot!

Between them, Howard Garton and Pat did excellent post-production work and the video was soon on the market. A few years later when the VHS video tape market started to fade Howard advised us to have it re-mastered into DVD format. That DVD, *Visitors from the Other Side*, is still available, and we know it has helped so many people to understand what took place in the circle.

As time passed, we were invited down to the South West of England, the South East and Wales. The next five years were very busy ones; including us taking up an invitation to speak and teach in Portugal when Tom had turned eighty.

He was a brilliant speaker, but even more importantly a good communicator – enthusing many to start their own circles. He was one of the very few people left in our world who really knew about and had years of experience in physical mediumship. He cared about people and for people. All across the world there are people who say their lives have been changed by his work and his caring.

However, in October 2010, after ninety-two years, he earned his 'promotion' and took his leave of us. Following a blow to the head in a fall at 2am on the morning of Friday 22nd he slipped into a coma from which there was no return.

\* \* \* \*

Coming home, for me, was going to be hard. My loving support system had gone, but I hadn't bargained for what he would be up to. The usual words we utter after a death are –

'Rest in Peace', but not for him; not a time now to sit back, and enjoy a well-earned rest to recover his strength after ninety-two years on this planet. Just seventeen hours after he had departed this world, during the Sunday morning service at the *Acacia Centre for Spiritual Awareness* in the Murcia region of south-east Spain, he made his presence known. He had returned not with an identifiable 'message' as such, but to make himself recognisable by the description given via the medium.

Robert and Barbara McLernon, who own the Centre had been good friends of ours for some years, so knew Tom well.

During the service, the clairvoyant medium sensed and described a man who was very strong in his manner. She knew he had become frail towards the end of his life; he was someone who was a very spiritual man and had been involved in Spiritualism most of his life; he would speak about it when he could and people liked to listen to him speak. She tried to get various people in the assembly to accept this information, but they could not relate to the person she was describing.

Rob eventually told her he knew someone like that and that the contact must be for him. The medium, then went on to describe the lady who had come with the man and Rob recognised her as Tom's mother. The medium followed this by saying "and as I leave you there's Agnes that has 'just popped in'." The icing on the cake – for this was a phrase that Tom said his Aunt Agg often used when she took Minnie in to trance and 'popped in' to tell them something.

Robert and Barbara were among the first people I had told of his passing the previous evening. Rob said to me at the time "He'll be back! Perhaps not tomorrow but he will."

Although the medium knew Tom slightly, she did not link the contact with him because no one there knew that Tom had died the night before. Robert had kept it a secret until after the service. Everyone knew we were on holiday in England for a month but not that anything was amiss. So it was that I received a very excited phone call from Rob that Sunday afternoon: "He's been through! He's been through!"

The inevitable physical separation had happened, but our work still had to go on. We had spoken of this many times and now it was up to me to carry on. Now it was my turn to tell all who would listen of the inevitability of survival of the human spirit. Only now, it would not only be based on what Tom had witnessed in their circle but also on what I have experienced during our life together. – And the first 'talk' was to be in exactly one week!

Tom had been invited to give his talk during the 'Stewart Alexander and Friends' October seminar at the Cober Hill Hotel on the North Yorkshire coast – so why not?

After all, I had been in training for this for seventeen years! At least it was to be on home territory, surrounded by friends. The energy in the lecture hall, that Sunday afternoon was amazing and with the support – from spirit friends and my listeners – I was on a 'high' whilst speaking and the allotted time just flew by.

Instead of dinner that night the hotel put on a superb buffet supper, and we celebrated the life and our memories not only of Tom, but also of Ernie Crone – another regular attendee at the seminars. Ernie had passed two months earlier, and his wife was present that weekend. That evening we also included a good friend of many there, Professor David Fontana, who had died five days before Tom. It was a wonderful party, which is what Tom had wanted. We drank a toast to them all, with the same brand of 'champagne' which Tom and I had enjoyed at a wonderful fund-raising evening for a small theatre just three weeks earlier.

That evening at the party we were joined by our good friends Susan Farrow, the Editor of the deceased[1] *Psychic News* and Chris Eldon Lee, the radio programme producer. Sue travelled the 200-miles by train from London, and Chris came by car from Cumbria, a four-hour's drive, just for the evening – such was their esteem and love for Tom.

The evening was rounded off with Sue, an international musician, playing the piano in one of the lounges. Bradley Harris joined her, his wonderful tenor voice adding a vocal touch, and among the songs, Tom's favourite – our theme tune – *Love changes everything.*

To quote an old poem found amongst his mother's papers

> No funeral gloom my dears, when I am gone;
> Corpse-gazing; tears; black raiment;
> graveyard grimness;
> Think of me as withdrawn into the dimness, –
> Yours still – you mine; remember all the best
> Of our past moments – and forget the rest.
> Cremate my body then my dears.
> When I am gone;
> Think of my soul in realms supernal,
> Returning oft to earth from the Eternal;
> Yours still – you mine; united still in love
> Till God shall call you too, my dears – above.

---

1. Sue & the team kept the contact going with an on-line publication *Spirit of PN.*

*Two*

# Tom Harrison: ambassador of spirit

I can't think of a better way to start this book about a wonderful communicator than this beautiful tribute from Susan Farrow which was first printed in Roy Stemman's *ParanormalReview.com* 'blog' the day following Tom's death.

**Date: Oct 24, 2010**

*Tom and Ann Harrison, May 2008*

News that an old friend, Tom Harrison, was in hospital and in a deep coma reached me late last week from Sue Farrow, the former editor of *Psychic News*. And within an hour or so of his passing, it was Sue, again, who conveyed the sad news to me. Despite her knowledge of survival, Sue found it difficult to suppress her emotion when we spoke on the phone. She has long been a close friend of Tom and his wife, Ann (pictured above), so I have invited Sue to use my blog to pay tribute to Tom and tell us about just a few of his contributions to Spiritualism, and why his passing is such a loss.

### The man who spoke for an unconventional truth

By Susan Farrow

The Spiritualist movement is infinitely poorer today for the passing of Tom Harrison, one of its most tireless and dedicated ambassadors.

Tom, who passed peacefully on 23rd October at the age of 92, had been admitted to hospital the previous day following a brain haemorrhage, thought to have resulted from an earlier fall. Though in a deep coma, he was in the company of his beloved wife Ann, daughter Wendy and son Alan.

What can one say of a man who spoke for an unconventional truth without fear or favour for more than seven decades?

Spiritualism was in Tom's blood. He was born into a Middlesbrough Spiritualist family on 8th August, 1918. His mother, Minnie, would later become one of the world's most powerful materialisation mediums, a fact that would influence the entire course of Tom's life in ways he could never have imagined. His Aunt Agg, Minnie's sister, was a respected trance medium, and was one of the mediums who gave the legendary Arthur Findlay some of the outstanding evidence contained in his revolutionary book, *On the Edge of the Etheric.*

On 2nd April 1940, while home on leave from the British Expeditionary Force stationed in France, Tom married Doris Hudson. They had become friendly in their teens through a shared association with the local Spiritualist Lyceum. Together they had six children - Colin, Mavis, Joyce, Alan, Derek and Wendy.

From 6th April 1946, Tom and Doris were part of a unique home circle known as The Saturday Night Club, a small group of family, friends and occasional fortunate guests who witnessed wonders that Spiritualists of today can only dream about. From that time, until the passing of Minnie Harrison, Tom and his fellow circle members were privileged to meet and talk with literally hundreds of materialised spirit people, all completely visible in good red light in the small back room of a house in Middlesbrough.

In his own words: "[They returned] not as fleeting, passing visions in somebody's mind, not even as wispy, transparent ghosts or spectres. They returned in fully-functioning, warm, heart-beating physical bodies. They returned and spoke with the same-sounding voices you would recognise. They returned with the same laughter, the same personality; and as you thrilled to feel their arms embracing you, and even kisses from their lips - the same love."

In 1958 Minnie Harrison lost her battle with cancer and the remarkable sittings of the Saturday Night Club came to an end. Tom lamented the loss of his mother, to whom he was very close, and also the loss of the extraordinary physical contact with the spirit world they had enjoyed for so long. The following year, he and Doris moved south to the village of Eton Wick, near Windsor so that Tom could take up a job as national manager of an engineering company. Four years later change was in the air again, and they embarked on the ambitious project of opening a restaurant in Cornwall. The restaurant thrived, Tom and Doris felt settled and content, and planned to put down roots. The spirit people had other ideas...

In 1966, the weekly Spiritualist newspaper *Psychic News* carried an advert for a founder manager to run the newly-created Arthur Findlay College at Stansted. Tom had long felt there was a need for a centre where people could come and study Spiritualism and psychic science, and immediately applied for the job. His application was successful, and the Harrison family was once again on the move.

Committed as ever to his work for spirit, Tom had expected to remain in the job for many years, but it was not to be. As he later wrote, "...a most unpleasant political intrigue caused great managerial problems" and though, urged by the spirit people, he agreed to stick out the situation a little longer, by 1968 things had reached an *impasse* and the family returned to Eton Wick. "I was terribly disappointed," Tom wrote, "but feeling so much happier away from all the unpleasantness at the College at that time."

Back on the job market, he returned to his former company, eventually becoming manager of their accounts office. Doris passed to spirit in 1976 at the age of just 59, a huge loss to Tom and his children, but he continued to travel the country, speaking about his mother's mediumship, and working as a freelance accounts adviser.

Meanwhile, another physical medium was busy developing in a home circle in Yorkshire. Stewart Alexander had heard of the amazing events which had taken place through Tom's mother's mediumship and decided to write to him. The two men came face to face for the first time in 1991 at a meeting of the *Noah's Ark Society for Physical Mediumship*. They formed a strong and enduring friendship, culminating in Tom becoming a member of Stewart's home circle. [Tom

*Clockwise from top: Ray Lister, June Lister, Susan Farrow,
Ann Harrison, Stewart Alexander, Gladys Shipman and
Tom Harrison*

is pictured, front row left, with Stewart Alexander and members of his circle, as well as Gladys Shipman, who along with Tom was the only surviving member of his mother's home circle, The Saturday Night Club.]

Stewart tells me that he is extremely sad at Tom's passing and thanks him for his "long, unwavering friendship". He adds: "For several years we were highly honoured to have both Tom and Ann Harrison as members of our circle. Following their relocation to Spain in January 2000 they became honorary members, visiting the circle whenever they were back in the UK. To say that Tom was a deeply valued friend who's wise, gentle counsel and support we were extraordinarily blessed to have, would be an understatement."

Tom and Ann had married in 1998 and found great happiness and contentment together. Even as Tom's health became increasingly fragile following the onset of Parkinson's disease, he continued undeterred to spread word of the wonders he had witnessed through his mother's mediumship, and in this he was enormously supported by Ann, who cared for him with extraordinary love and devotion. He once said to me that she had become so involved in his work that she now knew more about his life than he did!

In later years, Tom and Ann would share the platform during Tom's talks and lectures, he telling his story and Ann sitting at her laptop illustrating it with many of the remarkable photos that were taken during Saturday Night Club sittings. Only seven weeks ago he delivered that talk during the annual J.V. Trust[1] Week at Stansted Hall, at the invitation of J.V.'s chairman, Eric Hatton, who had known Tom for many decades.

"The passing of Tom to the spirit world leaves a void which will be difficult, if not impossible, to fill," Eric told me. "He was the epitome of everything a Spiritualist should be. He radiated spirituality and gentleness to all whom he touched, those being facets of a personality cultivated through a lifetime of close contact with the spirit world, largely through the remarkable mediumship of his mother, Minnie.

"My association with Tom goes back to the early days of Stansted Hall when, as the first manager, he showed leadership and restraint during the period when the College came into being and needed a dedicated hand on the tiller to see it through rough seas. By virtue of his nature and wisdom, Tom played a considerable part in ensuring that Arthur Findlay's dream became a reality. I shall truly miss his friendship, but I shall reflect long upon the privilege I had in knowing him."

It has been my own great privilege to know Tom and Ann well in recent years and to hear many of Tom's

1. The JV Trust is a charitable trust set up by Roy & Christine Wandless to aid spiritualists and is named after 2 of their children.

extraordinary experiences from his own lips. His recall of events that took place so many years ago was as clear as crystal, and his integrity and honesty shone brightly, leaving not a shadow of doubt that he spoke the truth.

As the late Professor David Fontana [whose passing we also reported just a few days ago - Roy] wrote in his introduction to Tom's 2004 book, *Life After Death: Living Proof:* "Tom is a man of transparent integrity, with no ambition for personal status or reward. His only interest in recounting the experiences he had with his home circle is to share with us the total conviction these experiences have given him of the reality of life after death. This conviction has left him with a deep humility and a spiritual presence that endears him to all those who meet him."

There is no doubt that Tom will have made a swift and easy transition to the next world, for if ever there was one who knew where he was headed, it was Tom. It goes without saying that he will have been met by a joyous company of loved ones and friends, all eager to welcome home a true pioneer of spirit."

Here are a few of the responses to Sue's article in paranormal review.com

*Frank* 24/10/2010 8.46pm

A wonderful tribute to a wonderful man, Susan

*Marion* 25/10/2010 2.06pm

Tom inspired me to reach for the higher truth, and the way he worked for many years with full materialisation with his mother and the rest of the group. We wrote and spoke, and this is what he said:

"We certainly had wonderful evidence every week for all those years. Unfortunately, there is no one we know of who has such clear materialised evidence but hopefully someone will come along in the future."

This is my hope also ...to get back to the way it was conducted long ago. What we have today is only a fraction of what was. Tom and his knowledge shall surely be missed.

Kind thoughts, Marion        (Edited by a moderator)


*Lynne* 25/10/2010 (in reply to Marion)

Tom also inspired me the same way. If I can't work in absolute truth, I will not work at all. This wonderful man taught me that and it will be my beacon always.


*Jo Winstone* 25/10/2010 08.05am

I am so sorry to hear of Tom's passing. He was one of the great, pioneering spiritualists and his like is sadly rarely seen today. Be happy with Minnie and Doris, Tom and thank you. God bless xx


*Bill* 25/10/2010

A wonderful tribute to a remarkable man. Thank you.


*Lis* 25/10/2010 01.46am

May I offer my thanks to Susan Farrow for such an informative, well-written and moving review of the life and passing to Spirit of Tom Harrison, a true pioneer of spirit.

The world is undoubtedly a poorer place for his departure and I am sure that all who knew Tom shall miss him dearly, but I am equally certain that his legacy will live on.

\* \* \* \* \*

A week later Sue's tribute was published again in *Spirit of PN*, the online version of the, by then, deceased *Psychic News*, under the editorship of Sue, who had been the editor of the paper when it was shut down. And here are some of the lovely words from readers there.

*Jay Love*  3/11/2010 5.19pm

I'm so saddened by Tom's passing....I'm sad because I did not get the chance to meet him And a little bit upset that spirit took him home just like that. What upsets me the most is we have lost such a wonderful man full of true understanding of the workings of physical mediumship some that is not witnessed today....Soon all the people that have witnessed true physical mediumship will all go home to spirit and leave the younger mediums to just read books on what was possible...The worst thing is there soon physical mediumship will be a thing of the past and that upsets me so much. However I wish you the best in your new life, Tom? How could I deny the spirit world a wonderful man like you Tom. I'll just have to read my books and live in hope physical mediumship will one day come back.....

*Jane Lyzell* 4/11/2010

A great man has passed to spirit – may your journey be joyful and happy – thanks for what you did for the Spiritualism and the movement:-)) – your wisdom will remain for ever.

Love Jane Lyzell
at the Spiritualist College Ramsbergsgarden, Sweden

*Terry Gardener*

We were privileged to hear and then meet Tom at Stansted many years ago. His lecture enthralled and inspired us. We went on to sit in and develop a wonderful home circle, in which we were able to witness some of the amazing things that he described all those years ago, and very often we spoke of our meeting with him. A truly wonderful ambassador for what he knew to be the truth ... his path to the light is assured!

*Norman Hutt* 4/11/2010 1.16pm

Tom's lectures were so inspirational. Having seen the ultimate proof for himself, he loved to share his knowledge. Another big loss to Spiritualism.

*Mickyb* 5/11/2010 8.52am

I had the privilege to meet Tom & Ann earlier this year. The meeting with them will stay with me forever, Tom & Ann gave me a book about Minnie Harrison it's a great read. My thoughts will always be with you both.

*Dave Haith* 21/11/2010 3,58pm

I met Tom many years ago as a newspaper journalist fascinated with survival of death and spent many hours chatting to him on the phone.

Then years later myself and a partner spent a wonderful evening with Tom and Ann delighting in Tom's recounting of his amazing experiences in physical mediumship.

Later we met Tom and Ann in Spain while we were on holiday.

I had the privilege of helping just a little with his book and secured a long interview for him on the Jeff Rense show on American radio – I still have the CD of that.

'Bon Voyage', Dear Tom – you really are a kind and gentle man always with a twinkle in your eyes and the warmest of hearts. No doubt he and his dear friend David Fontana are already chin-wagging over there!

*Andrew Russell* 28/11/2010

I had both the honour and the privilege of meeting Tom in May 1995 at Manchester Spiritualist Church, where his lecture on *Visits By Our Friends From The 'Other Side'* strengthened my interest in physical phenomena. Having spoken to Tom briefly after the lecture and posing several questions, he indicated he was pushed for time but assured me he would write to me with the answers to my questions. Sure enough, in a little over two weeks a letter arrived through the letterbox with those answers (which I still have along with the booklet from his lecture)!

Now how many people nowadays would do the same?!

Many thanks, Tom, you were an inspiration.

*Ann Prince* 29/11/2010 1.05pm

I was lucky enough to meet Mr Tom Harrison. He was a very kind, gentle and extremely generous man. Seeing the other comments, I know I was right in my estimation that he was a person of integrity.

I enjoyed the lecture that he gave.

*Three*

# Only Connect!

"Only connect! Only connect!"

The whole of one afternoon, in late July 2011, this phrase was running through my head, and I could not explain it. It felt familiar but from where? I began my search – it was not in the Oxford book of quotations, but an internet search soon traced it.

> Only connect! That was the whole of her sermon. Only connect the prose and the passion, and both will be exalted, and human love will be seen at its height. Live in fragments no longer. (E.M. Forster: *Howards End*)

But why was that constantly running through my head?

Two days later I received an email from Kate, a friend whose home circle we used to visit before we moved to Spain. She wrote:

> ... a few days ago I came home feeling tired and sat on the settee (twilight) wondering whether to put the TV on or have an early night, when a swirl of mist came towards me, from the ground upwards – it was about 3 feet in height. "Oh!" I said "I can see that, well done." - The mist settled at the right side of me and I said "Thanks for dropping in, friend, you are very welcome." I then could hear in my mind – "It's Tom." – "Oh wow! Very well done, Tom." I then kept getting, "Ann book, Ann book." and I said, "Yes bless her she is very busy with her books." The visit was not long and off I went to bed – so pleased that I had

seen the 'mist' and connected the 'mist' with a spirit person. The next day while cleaning up – back it [the voice] came again "Ann Book, Ann Book" and "Harrison connections." – "Yes," I said, "I will keep in contact with Ann don't worry." (thinking that this was what was meant). Later that day I went on the computer and oh my – the second line of your e-mail was 'there may be a book in it!'

My reply to Kate read: "Harrison Communications' that's a great title." But back came her email which told me that as she had read it, she sensed Tom saying – "NO! not 'communications' – Harrison Connections. ..."

Where do someone's connections begin? For we connect with others from the moment we are born and make links that may last for the rest of our lives.

Tom had a very special way of connecting with people. He loved being with them and, being a tactile person, a meeting, usually, finished with a hug at the very least – especially for the ladies. And he did once say to me, through Kate, that he found it "easier to communicate through a female energy than a male one – not that he was a ladies' man!!!" – No?! In the nicest way, with a twinkle in his eye, he enjoyed their company and they, his. He even 'adopted' one of his daughter's friends as a 'grand-daughter'. She was later a witness at our wedding.

Most of Tom's story has already been told in his book *Life After Death: Living Proof,* but some connections that led him to me, and so our life together, have remained hidden. Although I feel Tom means this book to be about his *post-mortem* connections, I do need to tell you of a few people who have, by their connection to Tom, also made a difference to both our lives.

Tom's later life was largely based around telling the story of his mother, Minnie's mediumship – thanks to Gordon Higginson's mother, Fanny. Having seen his circle photographs, she insisted 'he get out and tell people' about his experiences. But his life was much more than that.

He was very sensitive himself but would not use it to promote his own mediumship which he never sought to develop. In the early days, he knew he was the source of power for the circle, and then later accepted that it was his mission to tell everyone of the wonders he had witnessed. By his talks, he encouraged those who could, to develop their own gifts, and consoled those who were grieving with the assurance that their loved ones were not 'lost', nor sleeping but very much alive in the spirit world.

Tom's first love was giving healing, and he helped many people in that way too, but he came 'alive' when he could describe the contact they had had with the 'Other Side'.

In 1988 – when, as he put it, he reached the 'end of his shelf life' – he started to write a booklet about the circle and the phenomena. The first printing of the booklet *Visits by our friends from the Other Side* was funded by the sale of ten 'last season's' evening gowns, – donated by the owner of a boutique, whose monthly accounts he did.

Launching the booklet at Stansted Hall during Open Week, May 1989, it was a runaway success. Although he had turned seventy, he responded to requests from all over the country to tell them of his experiences. He loved to be able to do so, driving many miles, with the energy of a man much younger than his years; illustrating his talk with slides of

*The book launch at the Arthur
Findlay College Open Week with
Gladys Owen and Vi Kipling*

the photographs they had taken in the circle. *Psychic News* then undertook to sell the yellow-covered booklet and so friends were made all over the country and beyond.

The first of the important links formed because of the booklet was with Stewart Alexander. Sue Farrow has already described briefly how their friendship developed through the *Noah's Ark Society* and how Tom and I later became regular members of Stewart's Home Circle. But before the Society was even formed, Stewart bought a copy of the booklet.

Then, because he was building up his own personal archive on physical mediumship, he wrote to Tom requesting a copy of the *Christmas Party* recording. (Stewart tells me he still has a letter from Tom, dated September 1989.)

The recording at that time was only on an old seven-inch-reel, and it took some months before someone

*Stewart Alexander*

was found to transfer it to cassette. This request eventually led to Tom recording an introduction to an edited version of the original recording and having a cassette[1] produced for sale.

In 1993, Tom was invited to sit in Stewart's Home Circle and later, in the five years before we moved to Spain we were privileged to be full-time members of the circle and witness wonderful phenomena.

Our visits to England were always built around a date when it was convenient for us to sit with the circle. Often, this was also for Tom to give his talk to enthralled audiences at the Stewart Alexander reunions at Cober Hill Hotel near Scarborough. After Tom had developed Parkinson's disease Dr Barnett, one of the circle's spirit team, made a point of materializing and giving him healing. For although he came to Tom each night in the sleep state, he said the physical transfer of healing energy was much more effective.

The hospital Tom was taken to when he had his fatal fall is only a few miles from Stewart's home. I contacted Stewart that morning, and he and his wife came to be with me at Tom's bedside. Throughout the two days, Stewart came in a number of times so I might have a short break. During the last of these, he told me he had said his 'Goodbyes' and I'm certain Tom would hear him. Although Tom was in a coma, we know, that hearing is the last of the senses to go. Two hours later Tom slipped away.

This friendship was a most precious connection for us all.

Mr Millard Lindley, a ninety-year-old gentleman in Sheffield, contacted Tom after buying the booklet through *Psychic News*. When Tom learned of his situation and loneliness, he took to driving the 160 miles from Buckinghamshire to visit him once a month. Tom was able

---

1. Now available as a CD *The Christmas Party sitting 1954* -see *Bibliography*.

to get him some help to look after his flat, and in gratitude he left Tom his wonderful collection of books, papers and letters when he died in 1996. Many of these have been of invaluable help to me in research and to bring books back into print. Mr Lindley's cousin who was clearing the flat also gave us the bookcase they were in – very special mementoes for us.

David Haith, whose tribute you have already read in the previous chapter was another who bought his book through *Psychic News*. He was then a reporter for a local newspaper. Because he was fascinated by the paranormal he often used to 'sneak' a story or two into the paper and Tom was one of the first people he would phone for a quote.

*David Haith*

Dave told me, "From the start I found him to be compellingly honest and although his experiences were utterly over the top in many respects, I always believed he had seen what he had seen.

Tom was one of those special 'one-off' people with a warm, gentle energy and a great sense of humour behind those sparkling eyes."

David had indeed put Tom in touch with the American broadcaster Jeff Rense and because of the time difference with America we had to be by the telephone at 4am for the three-hour broadcast in February 2004. This led the following month to a broadcast on Richard Syrett's Canadian radio programme with Michael Roll and Gwen Byrne. The following year in April 2005 he was talking to Barry Eaton on radio in Australia. Remember Tom was by then eighty-five-years-old but he had amazing energy where spirit work was involved.

*Derek Ingram*

Derek, who lives near Basingstoke, wrote to Tom for a booklet, having seen an advertisement for it in Michael Roll's publication *Campaign for Philosophical Freedom*. He then went to see Tom for answers to his mountain of questions.

Derek told me he could see as Tom spoke that just talking about it rekindled the fire. Tom 'dug out' his memorabilia and 'became alive'. The desire to be able to sit again had been rekindled. They became firm friends. In 1993, knowing that Tom travelled to Yorkshire to sit with Stewart Alexander, Derek showed him an article in a spiritual magazine about a new centre in East Yorkshire – 'Fir Trees' – which he thought Tom could possibly visit.

He did, and three months later he returned to give his talk – and there we met ... I've always said it was all Derek's fault, Bless him!

Derek also corresponded with Shirley Wardell, who lived on the outskirts of Hull, about five miles from me, and whom I had met once at the small spiritualist church I attended in Hull. She had permission from Leslie Flint, the Direct Voice medium, to supply duplicated copies of his voice recordings, for a small

*Shirley Wardell*

donation to a local children's hospice. Derek had bought a number of tapes from Shirley and told Tom about her. Tom mentioned to me that he would like to meet her. So, as friends of hers were coming to our New Year's Eve party I asked them to invite her too.

Another beautiful connection was formed, and when Shirley passed with cancer a few years later, she gave all her copies of the tapes to us. We then undertook to continue to supply good copies to many people and raised several hundred pounds for the hospice, until we moved to live in Spain, when we stopped duplicating them.

I did, however, transfer all the cassettes we had to digital format so I had them preserved before they deteriorated further, and I can play them whenever the occasion arises.

When, in 1995, Tom moved north to be with me he turned to Derek for help. Derek drove the hired Transit van full of Tom's furniture up from Buckinghamshire, and that evening we treated him to his first physical séance with Stewart Alexander. His father spoke through Stewart and begged forgiveness from Derek, for not being there when Derek was small.

Contrition and forgiveness are absolutely essential before a spirit can make any progress in the world of spirit. So, in case we are not fortunate enough to be able to contact those wronged ones through a medium, it could be better to do it before we go over – however hard it might be to say the words.

Because of Shirley's gift to us, Marjorie, on the south coast, having seen an advertisement in *Psychic News*, wrote to us for some Leslie Flint tapes. A beautiful correspondence developed and we found that she and her husband had cared for the author Anthony Borgia in his later years. One of his books, *Life in the World Unseen*, had been my introduction to the world of spirit. I love his books, which were received clairaudiently from 'Monsignor' in the spirit world. In fact, her letters to us were written on the typewriter Anthony Borgia had used for the books.

'Monsignor' was, in life, Robert Hugh Benson and Anthony Borgia, an apt music pupil in the choir school at Westminster Cathedral, came into frequent contact with him during his years there. Later 'Monsignor' materialized during a séance to ask Anthony to help right a wrong he had done when he wrote his anti-Spiritualist book, *The Necromancers*.

*Audrey & David Bartlett*

Audrey, in the Midlands, also wrote wishing to buy copies of the Flint tapes and a fruitful correspondence developed. She and her husband David were interested in experimenting with EVP.[1] They also loved to listen to BBC Radio 4. One evening they heard a broadcast called *What Granddad did in the Dark*. This was a programme in which three granddaughters 'learned' about their grandfather, Noah Zerdin and his work with Leslie Flint.

Audrey was so impressed with the broadcast that she wrote to the Producer, and later sent his reply and a copy of the broadcast to Tom, She suggested that, if Tom got in touch with the Producer, he might make a programme about Tom's experiences.

---

1. EVP stands for Electronic Voice Phenomena (see p.264)

Tom did indeed get in touch with the producer, Chris Eldon Lee. That contact resulted in us going to Shrewsbury to meet him. Eventually the Radio 4 programme *Christmas Spirits* was made, with excerpts from the original recording of the 1954 Christmas Party séance. A former BBC technician also safely preserved the fragile 7 inch reel-to-reel spool as a digital recording.

*Chris Eldon Lee recording the 'Christmas Spirits' programme with Tom*

The programme included interviews with Circle members, Gladys and Sidney Shipman, and visitors, Gwen Schlegel and Don McKenzie, who had been at the circle that night. Don's father had made the original recording in January 1954. The programme went out on BBC Radio 4 on the 50th anniversary of that only recording of a Minnie Harrison Christmas Party séance.

This friendship with Chris resulted, not only in the broadcast and, six years later, shortly before Tom's 91st birthday, Tom performing a spiritualist blessing at Chris' marriage to Hannah, but also in Chris' introduction to Stewart's home circle. Chris continues to be a very welcome visiting sitter, and has had his first late wife, Sue and her vicar-father come to speak to him. One of Chris' visits 'just happened' to be the evening of Tom's first return to Stewart's home circle on 16th November 2010, three weeks after his passing. Chris was well able to recognise Tom's voice when he spoke to him directly – but more of that later.

*Prof. David Fontana*

Professor David Fontana, the psychical researcher, bought an early copy of one of Tom's small booklets. Some years later, in 1995, when invited to the Arthur Findlay College as part of the Experimental Week course, he heard, during an extra evening session following the talk, Tom answering questions about his mother's mediumship. When he saw the booklet, his excitement at meeting Tom was wonderful to see. He monopolised him for the rest of the evening. He had so many questions. He described the feeling between them as being like 'blood brothers'.

As President of the prestigious *Society for Psychical Research* (SPR) in 1996, David invited Tom to give his talk for them. He held Tom in such esteem that he travelled down from Cardiff to London specifically to chair the meeting – travelling back to Cardiff that same evening because of commitments the following day.

Eight years later when Tom asked David if he would write the Foreword to his new book David was delighted. Having seen my work in producing Tom's book, David asked me to do one for a colleague of his, on special needs education in the third world. He later also suggested that I might be able to help Anabela Cardoso with the publication of the journal for her ITC (Instrumental Trans-communication) organisation. This request has led to a good

*Dr Anabela Cardoso*

connection with Anabela, who lives in north-west Spain, and another method of communication for Tom to try out.

Two years later, David contacted me again, inquiring if I would be interested in publishing Louie Harris' complete manuscript of Alec Harris' mediumship. This led to a lovely visit for us to meet Bradley Harris, Alec's son. In 2010, Bradley had agreed to come and speak of his memories with his father at the Cober Hill October seminar. It was so good to have him there to add his wonderful tenor voice to the celebrations for Tom, David and Ernie – accompanied, as I have already said, by Sue Farrow on the piano.

At the time of his passing, David was negotiating with the SPR Council to get the SPR's *Proceedings on The Scole Report* back into print through our SNPP publishing house. This was finally achieved with the help of other SPR colleagues. The book, which meant so much to David, who was one of its authors, was launched on 5th November 2011 at the SPR's Study Day in memory of him.

Kate, near Doncaster, had bought her copy of *Visits by our friends from the Other Side* to make up an order from *Psychic News*, so when she saw an announcement for Tom's talk in Rotherham in 1995 she came along.

At the end of his presentation, Tom announced that if anyone knew of someone needing funds for the relief of cancer would they get in touch with him. She was nervous about approaching someone whom she saw as 'that great man'. But

*Kate Maesen*

she swears, to this day, that from the screen showing the picture of the Saturday Night Club group she saw Minnie nod her head and give a hint of a wink as encouragement – TWICE.

Kate and friends were helping to raise a vast amount for a mammogram scanner and a consultation suite for the hospital where she worked – a daunting task. Tom gladly made a donation from the sales of his booklet. They made their target and more.

As a result of that connection, we sat with her regularly, only losing contact for a short time, when she moved to the Blackpool area, and we were already living in Spain.

Contact is, however, now re-established and I am able to sit with her occasionally. But Tom is connecting with her whenever he wishes, and the Saturday Night Club circle are working with her, from their side, to develop physical mediumship again.


Another, very special, link was made not because the person had bought the booklet but because of all the other people who had. All the profits from it are dedicated to helping individuals who were suffering from cancer and needed help, or to the small groups who supported those people.

Tom did not give to large national research groups, preferring to work closer to home, where £100 would provide taxis to the hospital for treatment or funds for a support nurse to go when needed. On this occasion, it was a notice in the local paper which caught his eye, shortly after we had moved to Brayton, near Selby in North Yorkshire.

A local healing group was trying to form a support group for cancer sufferers, and the inaugural meeting was to be held in a nearby health centre a few days later. We went along and when invited to speak Tom told them he had not come to offer 'visiting' help, but financial support of £200 to get them going. He spoke to the two instigators later and, as we seemed to be on the same wavelength, invited them to come to our home for a chat. Our link was stronger than expected. It turned out that I already knew the sister of one of them. I had been in a group, under her leadership, giving spiritual healing, by 'laying-on-of-hands', to those who attended the special healing evenings at the spiritualist church I attended in Hull.

At that social evening in our new home, they suggested that we should get to know Geoff Everatt, one of the stalwarts of the local community, who had helped and instructed them; leaving us with his phone number the rest was up to us.

As we knew no one else in the area, there was nothing to lose. We telephoned him and after we had explained our conversation with the

*Geoff Everatt*

ladies, he invited us to call round the following week. The connection with Geoff was instantaneous, and we became close friends, with him often dropping-in for a cup of tea.

His introduction to the spiritual side of life had been a sitting with the medium Helen Duncan at which an uncle of his had materialised. He took his father to a later séance and there Geoff's half-brother Harold, who had been lost at sea, in the early months of the war, materialised, as did the lad's mother, Geoff's father's first wife. What evidence!

Geoff went on to sit with Leslie Flint, the Direct Voice medium; to witness healing with many excellent healers including Ronald Beesley and Harry Edwards; to study *Silva*

*Mind Control* amongst other things, and was himself a good healer.

As well as this side of his nature, he was a good businessman with a successful furniture store, and through this became involved in the furnishing of the Sanctuary at Findhorn with its founder, Eileen Caddy. He was a practical man and he loved to help with jobs particularly involving wood. He had the wood for my arbour cut to size, and put it up in our garden with Tom as his assistant. When we finally bought the house in Brayton, having rented it for a year, we decided to carpet the open treads of the staircase. Geoff insisted on cutting the batons and wood for the 'risers' and fitted them. He then 'supervised' the fitting by the carpet fitter from his own furniture business, as well as acting as 'mate' to help with laying the carpet.

*Having taken a photo of our villa Geoff, added a copy of a picture of us in the window and himself flying in on a broomstick to visit. Such was his wonderful sense of humour. Why a broomstick? - 'Broomsticks' was the name given by a sceptical husband to the group we taught at La Manga Club and we had taken Geoff there on one of his visits to Spain.*

When we moved to Spain, although he was in his late eighties, he visited us several times but stopped flying when he turned ninety. He was insatiably curious and constantly experimenting on his computer with aspects of the Photoshop software of which I still have no clue. The photo opposite is one of his early 'Photoshop' compositions after a stay with us in Spain.

He was another friend we made sure we saw on our trips home – and he was one of the people we visited on Tom's final day before the fall. But Geoff didn't have too long to wait for a reunion, as he too died just nine months later.

On one of our final trips to visit him, I was privileged to be given a wonderful gift – his treasured copies of the books written by Dr Macdonald Bain. He was a spiritual teacher and trance medium whom Geoff admired, and who had spoken to him through the Direct Voice mediumship of Leslie Flint.

Early in 2004 we hit the problem of getting Tom's new book published. None of the mainstream publishers were interested and although David Fontana recommended his publisher they too turned us down. To them, Tom was unknown – but help was at hand.

Tom and Lisa Butler, the EVP researchers from Arizona, were then the Directors of the Dept. of Phenomenal Evidence for the American National Spiritualist Association of Churches and also the American Association AA-EVP. recently renamed Association of TransCommunication as they now cover more than just voices on tape recordings.

*Lisa & Tom Butler*

Having seen an item about Tom's booklet on a website Lisa contacted the website owner, and he forwarded his reply to Tom. In the ensuing e-conversations with the Butlers, it turned out they had hit the same problem with their book, *There is no Death: There are no Dead.* They had solved it by self-publishing through the internet. Tom Butler told us about the company they had used to print the book and gave us help with suggestions as to how to go about it. Another connection was born and by it the means to get Tom's book into print, but this time it was also a connection for me to the world of ITC.

The connection with this printing company was to give me a new all-absorbing pastime and now – after twenty-five books – more like a career.

We did meet Tom and Lisa in person a few weeks later, in Vigo, in the north-west tip of Spain, at the ITC Journal Conference, which David Fontana was helping Anabela to organise.

The list could go on and on, but I have tried to concentrate here on those connections that came about because of his booklet. Six of those dear friends are now also in the spirit world, and no doubt have met up, but my connections to Stewart, Derek, Dave, Chris, Kate, Anabela and Tom and Lisa still continue.

There are now connections made because of the new book, and one of those deserves a special mention. Manfred Poser, in Germany, having read Tom's book, wrote to him and also spoke with him on the telephone. Manfred had been asked to write a chapter for a German book about paranormal phenomena, and he wished to include the chapter from Tom's book about the first encounter with the materialised form of Aunt Agg. Tom immediately gave his permission, but the publishers got cold feet and the book was never published. In February 2012, Manfred contacted me asking if he might translate the whole book of Tom's book into German as he had already done one chapter. I happily agreed, and one year later it was published, much to the delight of Kai Mügge, the German physical medium, who was another of Tom's email connections, who wrote to Tom after he had read *Life After Death: Living Proof.*

When the new book was published, we decided to let the little yellow booklet go out of print, as all the material was in the new book. As supplies ran out, I heard from some people that they were dismayed there were no more copies. They had been in the habit of buying several at a time, to give to people they came across, who needed the help and understanding it gave. So in February 2011, having included the loose extra pages which used to be tucked into the back, I brought it back into print, with the cover looking the same as it did twenty-two years before.

So, thank you to everyone who has bought the booklet whether you have been in touch or not. Your contributions have helped so many cancer sufferers, as I continue to use the profits from both books in the way Tom did.

*Four*

# Iberian Connections

These next two important connections involve the Iberian Peninsula – that is Spain and Portugal or chronologically Portugal and Spain.

### Like a long-lost brother!

In September 1998, Tom saw a letter in *Psychic News* offering a warm welcome and three nights' hospitality to anyone who would go to Portugal, and teach a small group of spiritually interested people, at the eastern end of the Algarve.

We decided it would be new ground, so Tom wrote to *Psychic News* offering our services. The resulting telephone calls, and discussion of what we could offer, resulted in a suggestion to meet up. But where? We were in England, and Valerie and Frederick Smith were in Portugal.

Frederick's son had died of cancer in 1993, and that had been the catalyst for his investigations. He started going to a few mediums to try to see if Scott would come through. They became interested in healing; organized groups and ran services across the Algarve. Later Frederick developed trance mediumship, which he now teaches.

During my visit to their villa near Moncarapacho in July 2013, I asked Frederick and Valerie to think back to that first meeting. It was a long time to think back, but we had first met in December 1998. Tom and I had married in the May;

Tom was eighty in the August, and we went out to South Africa for Christmas that same year.

Frederick recollected:

> Well, having spoken to Tom on the telephone we agreed that we ought to meet but it was difficult with us living in Portugal and you being in England. As we tried to find a date, Tom said 'Well, we are going away for Christmas. We'll be in South Africa near Jo'burg.' To which I replied 'What a coincidence! We are not going to Jo'burg, but we will be at Pretoria.' And Tom said 'Pretoria's not far and we could come and meet you,' so that was set up.
>
> Having driven that day from Hazy View near the Kruger National Park to Pretoria – that in itself was quite an experience – we arrived at the Victoria Hotel, which was like stepping back a hundred years. On the closed-in verandah round the outside of the hotel you could imagine people having their afternoon tea at the turn of the last century.

I remembered it so well, all the dark wood and the wicker chairs, overlooking the old main street and the Railway

*On the verandah of the Victoria Hotel, Pretoria, South Africa, 1998.*

Station from which they were to leave the next morning *en route* to Victoria Falls.

Frederick continued reminiscing:

> And we went outside and had tea, sitting on that closed verandah – the four of us. It was at that meeting where Tom actually brought through my son, dear Scott, who had been in spirit since October '93. He had been through to us through some physical mediums, but Tom didn't know anything about this. I had taken Scott's sun hat with me to South Africa, so the energy was there. When I put it on the table, Tom touched it and he immediately linked in …

I remembered so clearly how Frederick had gone back into their room, and brought out a man's straw hat which he placed on the table. That seemed to act as a trigger. Tom became deeply overshadowed by Scott and passed on a beautiful message and good memories to Frederick, which meant so much to both of them.

"He didn't do that very often." I reflected.

"No, he didn't push his mediumship, did he?"

"No he didn't."

After a few moments thought, Frederick continued:

> And when we met, like with so many other people, it was like meeting a long-lost brother. We always said Brother Frederick – Brother Tom. We used to use that phrase with each other – but he was that sort of a person, wasn't he? You couldn't help but suddenly feel that when you were with him. He had that way with him.
>
> So at Pretoria it was a wonderful meeting and from that point onwards you couldn't let that meeting just die, so we kept in contact. A unique person - Tom. …There are people who come to the earth plane with specific tasks to perform – those who do, perform them so well. He was special.

Valerie nodded: "Yes, he was."

I asked Frederick if he could remember anything specific that Tom said that day in Pretoria?

"No, I can't. I can only remember, it was amazing," was his response.

I reminded them "It was 27th December 1998 when we met in Pretoria, and we assumed we had met with your approval – because you had wanted to make sure that we were suitable. You weren't having any old so-and-sos coming over, saying they could teach, and taking your hospitality. It was arranged that we would come out in the second half of May, the following year, and we then we would go on to stay in Vilamoura."

"And that was your first anniversary," Frederick recalled. "We were thrilled when you said 'Would you like to come to dinner. It is our first anniversary.' We thought surely they don't want anyone around for their anniversary – the first one!"

During the first three days with Frederick and Valerie we were very busy. Tom gave his talk to their group. Then we did the workshops. I showed them how to use their energy, the basis of kinesiology, and how to get the energies moving. Another day we used dowsing rods and the Ouija board. Irene, one of their group, was excellent on the board, getting very accurate communication. On the fourth day they drove us to Vilamoura for the rest of our week's holiday, and that is where they joined us for our anniversary dinner in one of the local restaurants. A lovely memory.

While we were at Vilamoura, Tom decided that he wanted to go back there for three months of the winter to write his book so we would need an apartment. Tom had seen where he wanted to be, overlooking the sea – a source of inspiration to him. Valerie said she would look out for an apartment. On a flight back to England in the September, she met someone on the plane who had a place exactly where we wanted to be in the village next to Vilamoura. Valerie got in touch, to say that she had found somewhere for us, and we had to say – 'Well, thank you very much but we are going to live in Spain!' For in the September, only four months after our visit to Portugal, our friends in Brayton persuaded us to go to Spain to see their new holiday home. In those two weeks a house 'found' us and I 'knew' we had to be there.

Over the years, we have met up with Frederick and Valerie a good number of times, always feeling that there had been no time gap in our days together. We loved to visit them on the Algarve despite the long drive across Spain. In April 2008, we were the first visitors to stay with them at their new apartment in Eastbourne, and five months later they drove the 900 kilometres from the Algarve to be here, in Eagles Nest, at Tom's Spanish 90th birthday party.

A very special kinship connection.

### The Spanish Connection

When we moved to Spain in 2000, we did wonder what life had in store, but we knew, in all certainty, it was the right thing to do.

On our initial holiday in Spain, we had renewed contact with Edith Baker, who with her husband Ted had founded *The Baker Foundation Spiritual Centre* on the Costa Blanca, south of Torrevieja. We had first met her in 1996, when Tom had given his talk at her spiritual centre in Bath. Four months after that first visit to Spain we began working with her. One day she asked if we would mind travelling down to the exclusive development at La Manga Club to speak to a group of ladies who were interested. We were more than happy to do so, and our connection with what became known as the 'Broomsticks' continued for almost four years.

Just as the connection to Stewart was an important part of Tom's life – and mine – in the 1990s, this association led to a new connection. One which has been such an important part of our lives in Spain.

In May 2001, I had arranged for my friend Angela McInnes to visit Spain, to take services and give spiritual readings at the *The Baker Foundation*. During that week, we took her to La Manga Club to give readings to members of our group – with great success.

That weekend there was a party at the Club and Robert McLernon, newly arrived from Scotland, was taken as a guest of his hostess. There out of the blue, a lady, completely unknown to him, asked him if he was interested in healing. She then added that he should have been there earlier that week as they had had a medium from Scotland, and she was good. When she told him the medium's name, he could not believe it, as they had both been on the Spiritualists' Union Council for Scotland & Ireland some years before. When he telephoned us, Angela had already returned to Scotland, but we arranged to meet up when he was next out in Spain.

It was six months before we met, at another 'Broomsticks' day and as we introduced ourselves we could feel the overwhelming spirit presence of someone we all knew well. It was obvious that our meeting was an important moment in our spiritual work. However, a further seventeen months passed before we started to work together. By then Rob had met Barbara, and they were starting to look for a property, where Rob could expand his healing work and be able to do some teaching.

In the early days, the four of us started our circle sittings by using the Ouija board. One evening the planchette kept pointing to three numbers – the listed price (in thousands) of the house they should buy. As it finished moving, Tom was aware of a crown and a squat tower. I maintained that it wasn't a tower it was a windmill but Tom stood his ground.

They bought the house, which stood on a large plot of land, out in the 'campo' (countryside). At the end of the road leading to it, was a windmill and impressed in the tiles as you entered their gate was – a crown over a squat tower.

Clearly it was the right place, and we have worked together ever since.

In November 2008 they opened a Spiritual Centre in the building at the end of their garden. Services are held there every Sunday. There are frequent development courses, occasional special events with visiting physical mediums and a great deal of healing work.

*Left to right: Mrs Edith Baker with Barbara and Robert McLernon at the opening ceremony of the Acacia Centre for Spiritual Awareness, near Balsicas, in the Murcia region of Spain. Nov 2008*

This was the first place that Tom returned to after his passing, and he delights in making his presence known, particularly to help those trying to develop their mediumship skills.

Tom is always so close to us, that Rob, half-jokingly, said to one trainee medium before a service, "If you feel you haven't a contact just say – 'I've got Tom here,' because he will be!"

And Tom was there that morning. But more importantly for the young man, who knew Tom slightly and had read his book, he was given accurate information about which he knew nothing, but I was able to accept. A good boost for the young man's confidence.

Again a special, dare I say, pre-ordained connection. It certainly feels like it.

*Five*

# When God calls –
# a very special connection

From early summer, I knew that Tom was becoming more frail and unsteady. He was pushing himself to keep going; doing whatever he could; sorting his workshop – with the result I couldn't find anything. He would then rest, usually in our peaceful Sanctuary. From early July, occasionally, as he woke about lunch time, surprised that he had been asleep, he would say "I've been planning a trip, but I don't know where to." When I reminded him of the August trip to Arthur Findlay College, for him to give his talk, and then the October trip to the Cober Hill seminar, he would reply "Yes I know, but this is different."

In mid-September, he determined to start painting the garden wall extension. We had had two more rows of large concrete blocks put on the top of the existing wall for privacy and the rough grey cemented finish needed painting. As the weather started to cool, he would spend two hours a day painting; climbing up and down the step-ladder to reach the top. He made a good job of covering a very rough pebble-dashed surface.

Silently, I had asked of my spirit friends – "Great Spirit – whoever? How are you going to take him? You can't be meaning to let him go to the end of Parkinson's disease? He doesn't deserve that."

On Sunday September 19th, seventeen years to the day that we had met, Tom felt too tired to attend the Sunday service, so I went alone and Rob did have a short message for me.

Amongst other things, he told me that Norman, my first husband, who had died twenty years earlier, was very close. "He is always with you. There is an anniversary around now." (*Yes, for Tom and me but also the anniversary of my father's passing.*)

"There is a Jane. Norman has brought her in, a lovely sweet personality. She is saying 'It will be all right.'."

Jane, Norman's mother, had been bedridden, paralysed and blind for the last ten years of her life, after a stroke. The message from her 'It will be all right,' I felt was my answer about Tom. I was not to worry it would not be a drawn-out death.

I was not to know that it would be only five weeks away! – What a blessing we do not know 'the hour'. But it seems that the spirit does for he had been making contact on a soul level. Even before he had had his fatal fall, he was preparing.

It was not until I saw Annemarie at Cober Hill I knew of the amazing experience and involvement she had had in Tom's passing.

Here is Annemarie's story:

*Annemarie Lewis*

When you meet someone for the first time, it is very rare you are put at ease and made welcome. For me this encounter, at a *Noah's Ark Society* seminar at the Wakefield College in the early 1990s, hosted by Stewart Alexander and Tom, left an indelible mark upon my consciousness. One which has stayed with me since that incredible day, and it is this that brings us to October 2010.

I knew nothing about the subject then, nor was I a Spiritualist. However, Tom and I somehow made 'connections'.

He became a father-figure to me, and from that first meeting I had a healthy respect for him.

It was, therefore, a surprise to me that he was to make himself known to me in an altered state of consciousness. It had happened only once before – with my father, eleven years previously, at his transition.

At 2am, on a Friday morning, [eight days before his transition] I woke; I could not get back to sleep; I felt agitated and somewhat disorientated. I went downstairs to make a cup of tea. I know if I am disturbed in this way, 'someone, somewhere is pacing'. I was impressed to link in with this person to aid them in their disorientated state. I was not aware it was Tom until I had linked-in. I knew his health over the previous few months had given concern, but this was different. As I sat sipping my tea, I became aware of his distinct energy and I was mentally impressed to strike up a conversation, mind-to-mind.

His concern was that he was not sure where he was and asked for help. I suggested he look around and see where he was. When he got his bearings, he thanked me and was gone. I was then able to go back to bed. It was now 3am.

Over the next four days, every morning at 2am, I woke with the same feeling, but less disorientated. When I got up for a drink of tea, Tom was there in an energy-form, communicating mind-to-mind, each time was stronger than the initial contact. He specifically asked for help in the 'preparation side of things'.

By Tuesday, I was aware of what he had intimated, and he made me aware that he was waiting and wanted help.

The visits continued until the Friday, the day before his passing as it turned out. At 2am, he woke me again; I tuned-in. This time I met him in a room. The interior was all white, but the atmosphere was calm and relaxed. He stated that this was a waiting area. There were two doors, one at each end of this submarine-shaped pod. Benches either side. This time I felt as though I had astral travelled with him. He asked me to keep linking in with him as he was 'just waiting'. He was calm and not distressed in any way. It seemed important to him that he was making preparations.

All day Saturday, I was aware of him, on the one hand, he was nervous and apprehensive, but on the other he was ready to go. By 6.30pm, I was aware that the final struggle was over.

Sunday morning, I was again wakened by his presence, but it was different. So alive and exuberant; so radiant: "I am in a hurry, wake up; come with me." He took me to a theatre all gold and red, with boxes on either side. He told me to transform into a blue bird and hide behind a tall, ornate, golden column and watch everything from above. I saw the Hull Circle [the spirit circle] sitting in the royal box to the left. Tom was looking very smart in a tuxedo. On the stage were lots of people cheering and clapping. He was being presented with an award for all his hard work to do with Spiritualism. It was phenomenal.

He was stunned and overjoyed, and quite bemused. He looked at me and said, "Tell them when you go to Cober." (the Stewart Alexander seminar, the following weekend).

In the letter that Annemarie wrote later, she told me:

All this only made sense to me when I heard Annette speak. I feel very humbled that Tom chose me to do this. I hope this brings you comfort knowing he is still popping in and making his presence felt in such wonderful ways. Thank you, Tom and Ann for this. As I read this now, I feel I have completed the link, and am very emotional. I hope in the words I have written you can feel his energy. He wants you to pass it on as it might help others. Thank you for this opportunity to share this with you. I love you both very much. There are tears of joy and a feeling of gladness.

Annemarie

Dr Annette Childs, the psychotherapist/counsellor with the dying and the bereaved in America for over twenty years, gave the first talk at the Cober Hill seminar the weekend after Tom's passing.

As she described how people nearing death would say they had been 'waiting' or 'standing in line' (American for queuing), Annemarie and I could hardly contain ourselves. Before the talk Annemarie had already told me of how Tom had told her, he was 'waiting'.

Annette also told us another common phrase used as the person woke was – 'I've just been planning a trip' – as Tom had done for at least three months before his fatal fall.

Annette had written emails to Tom, the previous year after she had read his book *Life After Death: Living Proof.* In them she had told him how the book had opened – 'an aspect of life new to me', although she was used to, as she says, 'afterlife encounters' with her clients. I know she was looking forward to meeting Tom at the seminar. However, the key words in her talk gave both Annemarie and myself a wonderful insight into life before death, and what our souls are up to on a different level of consciousness.

Many months later Peter Egan, a wonderful speaker at the Cober Hill seminars, read this passage from Neale Donald Walsch's first book of *Conversations with God:*

> Now it happens often that the soul makes a decision that it is time to leave the body. The body and the mind – ever servants of the soul – hear this, and the process of extrication begins. Yet the mind (ego) doesn't want to accept. After all, this is the end of its existence. So it instructs the body to resist death. This the body does gladly, since it too does not want to die. The body and the mind (ego) receive great encouragement, great praise for this

from the outside world-the world of its creation. So the strategy is confirmed.

Now at this point everything depends on how badly the soul wants to leave. If there is no great urgency here, the soul may say, "All right, you win. I'll stick around with you a little longer." But if the soul is very clear that staying does not serve its higher agenda – that there is no further way it can evolve through this body – the soul is going to leave, and nothing will stop it – nor should anything try to.

The soul is very clear that its purpose is evolution. That is its sole purpose – and its soul purpose. It is not concerned with the achievements of the body or the development of the mind. These are meaningless to the soul.

The soul is also clear that there is no great tragedy involved in leaving the body. In many ways, the tragedy is, being in the body. So you have to understand, the soul sees this whole death thing differently. It, of course, sees the whole 'life thing' differently, too – and that is the source of much of the frustration and anxiety one feels in one's life. The frustration and anxiety comes from not listening to one's soul.

How right, for Tom has since told me he was tired of keeping going with his failing body.

Annemarie also told me that Tom had made reference to the *White Cliffs of Dover* and 'Vera Lynn'. She felt that somehow this was important for me.

Tom loved Vera Lynn's voice and her songs. We had bought two CDs of them only a few months earlier, but some years before I had drawn pictures of what turned out to be song titles, during a 'mediumship' exercise, not knowing who the recipient was to be. Tom was the only one in the group who could link with the six song titles and one of them was *'Blue birds over the white cliffs of Dover'*. He had that postcard in a silver frame on the shelf above his desk where he must have looked at it every day – as I now do.

*Six song titles drawn and given during a mediumship exercise.*

And if you finish that 'blue bird' line it says –

**'Just you wait and see!'**

*Six*

# Death is no barrier

Tom certainly demonstrated that 'death' was no barrier in his first few months, in the spirit world. Having found the renewed vigour of a man in his prime, he told me he did not need his spectacles; some of his hair was back; he was as in the 'old photo'. And he has very been busy connecting with some of the mediumistic people he had had contact with here.

He made at least two visits to Australia – to Melbourne and Sydney and to one 'sensitive' lady in Washington State, on the west coast of America. She sent an email in February saying she hoped he was well but had felt impelled to read his book for the fifth time. When I wrote to her that he was now in spirit, she replied that she had wondered if he was all right as she had found herself thinking of him from around early November.

In this chapter, I give you three very different contacts that happened in the first two weeks after his 'death'.

The seminars with Stewart and Friends at Cober Hill Hotel and Conference Centre in North Yorkshire are always wonderful weekends of laughter and camaraderie. A true linking of the two worlds; with meditation time; talks on various aspects of contact between the worlds; workshops and of course the physical séance on the Saturday evening. As well as these, there is plenty of time for socializing – catching up with old friends and meeting new ones.

The Saturday afternoon is the time for workshops. You can take a brisk walk down to the sea or a gentle stroll in the woodland garden, but the relaxed workshop atmosphere offers one a chance to try to improve a skill in communicating with the spirit world.

*October 30th, 2010:*

A workshop is what Gilly chose and, as in previous years, she joined one taken by Violet Eccles, for the development of mental mediumship. Violet makes a special journey from Melbourne, Australia to be at the seminar each autumn. I usually, join them. However, this year I excluded myself from all of them, needing time to prepare for the following day when I was to give Tom's talk for the first time on my own. I have done plenty of my own talks, but this one was special.

*Gilly Woolfson*

Here is what Gilly told me she was aware of during the workshop:

I have put my responses and additional explanations in italics as I was not present and they were added to Gilly's detail later.

As I closed my eyes to make a contact, the very first thing I heard was – "It's TOM," shouted loudly, distinctly and firmly; said twice, at the same level. He further impressed me by showing a picture of himself, as tall and sturdy – a dark-haired young chap – a vigorous feel. At your presentation the following day I saw the photograph of him in the Saturday Night Club and recognised it as the picture of him that I had seen the day before. He talked about a mark on his face.

*(Yes, he had a mark.)* – When we spoke afterwards I told her he had a scar from shingles, but Gilly did not feel this was right as she saw it as dark. I later saw there is a black mark on his forehead on the photo of the Saturday Night Club that I used in the Power Point presentation. Tom and I had never noticed this in all the years we had used this picture. It was only when I sent a copy of the picture to Gilly a few days later that I noticed it.

*Tom 1948: showing the mark on the group photo.*

Had he been with me and seen it while I was studying the slides in my room that afternoon? I think he must have been.

He talked about the army – again very strongly given.

*(He was seven years in the army – the whole of the war, and he had just been 'demobbed' when they started the Circle. He was also in the Army Reserve for a number of years after that.)*

He talked about 'Aluminium'; this was very loud, firm and strong. He repeated it three or four times and impressed me as being very important. At the time, I could not imagine what this was about but when I stood up to give my message he impressed me that it was a séance trumpet.

*(Yes, the old one we have is Aluminium.)*

There was a London connection – it came straight after Aluminium.

*(Yes, Aunt Agg was a medium in London, and it is her trumpet, used in London. Tom had shown Gilly that trumpet the year before when he had spoken with her about development.)*

Beaches – I saw a long, expanse of beach. I lived in by the sea in Cornwall for many years, and the picture was the one I loved too.

*(For three years he lived by the beach at Perranporth – a long beach he loved to walk. We have been back there on holiday.)*

<u>Strawberries</u>. This was strongly emphasised as important. I felt afterwards as I wrote these notes that it had to be underlined.

*(He did love them, but it was also the very last thing that he ate.)*

Beautiful garden / Landscaping – Firstly he showed me a picture of my garden, with low walls and roses etc., small steps. It felt like a personal garden, gardens you and he had created together, sunny and bright was the impression I had, and the overall enjoyment of seeing the gardens and being in them.

*(I have had beautiful gardens and Tom had helped with the landscaping in two of them, particularly in Spain as we started it from scratch. We have small steps there, and we loved to sit out in it with our morning coffee.)*

Marble Halls – pillars – they looked light, 'creamy' coloured, spacious and a high-ceilinged room.

*(The last time we were out with Wendy and Joyce, his daughters, – one week before he passed – we were in just such a place at Stoke Park Golf Club for lunch. Wendy had won this as a raffle prize at the Charity Evening, the previous Saturday.)*

"Love to Ann. My support and love are with her." He's so glad she is here – Always love.


Later when she wrote it down, she added – I felt his pride in you. There was also a reference to San Francisco. Gilly wrote that "it felt like a distant, future connection."

In the card that Gilly sent me few days later she also said:

As I stood to give out the message – and at the time I had not realised who I had with me – I said to the group and to Violet "I feel comatose." I felt heavy, hot and 'out of it'. It was a struggle to talk or move. As I gave the message, Tom made sure that I realised who was giving the message and how important it was to let you know he was with you at Cober. After the message I felt so ill that I had to excuse myself and go to my room to lie down.

*(That was his physical state before he passed.)*

Tom had fallen heavily, but we did not know it had caused an internal haemorrhage and during sleep he went into a coma. He did become very hot and was sweating when the paramedics arrived to take him to the hospital. Also at the very end, Wendy said he became hot again before passing – pneumonia was given as the cause of death.

The only part of Gilly's detail I could not connect with at the time was San Francisco. However, when I arrived home two weeks later, I found our friend John Finnemore, in California, had been the first to leave a message on our answer-phone in Spain. He had seen the report by Sue on Roy Stemman's *Paranormal Review* blog. John lives in Cupertino, so I checked the map, and I found that it is at the southern end of San Francisco Bay.

It was strange, but I wondered if anything else would come up around that. Two months later, on 30th December, I had a phone call from Gabriele, a friend of John's, also in Cupertino, who wanted a book in print by Feb 16th. I felt a good link between us, and I did manage to get the scholarly book, *Homochronos*, done in time. Were these the connections referred to when Gilly got 'San Francisco'? I believe so.

Following his talk at Cober Hill the previous year (2009), Tom had spoken with Gilly, advising and encouraging her on her mediumship development. Gilly later wrote this to me after she had contacted me about getting a trumpet:

When I asked Tom about my development, he advised me to be patient above all, and to let Spirit guide me as to my correct path, and keep to it – as they did all those years ago, to tremendous effect in the end. He advised me to get an aluminium trumpet – (as you did) – and as he said that he was holding Aunt Agg's trumpet with great reverence and fondness. He passed it to me to hold, and pointed out the dents from good use. It is interesting that almost his first words to me at Cober this time were 'Aluminium' and 'Trumpet'.

Thirteen good facts through Gilly, and one verified later – nothing incorrect.

In the same group, that afternoon was Belinda, who told me that she could see Tom's face in front of Gilly as she was speaking, and she heard "Love the flowers." Tom had had a private sitting with Belinda a few years earlier during one of the seminars, so they too had a connection.

The SNU Almoner had sent flowers to Cober Hill from the Spiritualists' Union, and I had received another bouquet of flowers through Eric Hatton on behalf of the SNU Benevolent Fund. Stewart and June had also had a yellow and orange (Sunshine) flower arrangement delivered to honour him at the seminar. So we had lots of flowers to decorate the table for the party on the Sunday evening.

It would have been too much to expect Tom to come through in the séance that Saturday evening. However, I did have a connection – our wonderful friend and guardian, Sunrise, made his presence known and you can read about it in Katie's report in the next chapter.

*November 6th 2010:*

A few days after the seminar, I went to stay with good friends for a short break – 'to gather strength' as they said, before returning home, and launching into sorting things out.

Their home is a haven of peace and I was glad to be able to unwind. Here too, I was to experience the love from the spirit world. Steve Barry is a good deep-trance medium and he decided, as all the circle were present, that they would sit to see who could draw near. Tom and I had sat with them once before, in our own home the previous May, when they were in Spain, on holiday with the couple who are the other half of their circle. And what a beautiful evening that had been.

On this occasion in Norfolk, we were joined in the circle by Steve's brother, who had never sat before, and what a joyous time we had again. After the prayer had been said, and the spirit friend who opens the proceedings had left, we heard a breathy sound: "aaaaaaah ..... Aaaaaaaaaaoooooo annnnnn. (Very light and breathy.)

> Weeeell ... Annnn ... Tom here. (Ann: Hello Darling, come on, I can hear you.) ... We believe it is easy bu...ut we know it's difficult..."
>
> Ann: Yes we know, we know. You are doing so well.
>
> Tom: You are my love. (A: Thank you and you mine.) ... Can't stay long ...
>
> A: No, I know. You are doing so well and it is so good to hear you – so good. ...
>
> T: Will you tell them ... Wendy, I'm with her mother. (A: Oh good!) She sends her love to you. (A: Thank you.) ... Love to all. We're just beginning.
>
> A: Yes, yes I'm sure.
>
> T: Tell Robert to look after you. (A: I'm sure they will.) Tell all of you to look after my girl.
>
> Sitters: We will, Tom, yes.
>
> T: Here it's beautiful, (A: Good.) – it's beautiful. (A: More than you thought?) Much, much more! (A: Good.) When ... when you go home... (*he starts to struggle with the voice*) (A: "Steady love, steady.) You know I've already been.

(A: You have?) Yes. (A: Everything all right?) Ye..es. We will help you; (A: Thank you.) – returning to help you. We are all together. Couldn't remember how everybody looked. (A: You couldn't? They look good?) Just as in the picture. (A, *laughing:* Lovely.)

(*The voice starts to change in accent.*) You have the old photograph? (A: Yes.) Talk to Wendy. (A. I will. I'll see her on Tuesday.) Have to go. (*a whistling sound as he fades*) (A: 'Bye for now, love.) Love to all.

All speaking together: "God bless you; well done."

We had spoken with Tom for over five minutes.

Within a few seconds, a young male (YM) communicator with a strong Midlands accent started to speak:

"You all right? You all right? "

All: Yes, thank you.

YM: It's all right, I had to pop in a little bit to help him. Ooh, he's a stiff old boy that Thomas, isn't he? He's a stiff old boy. He couldn't quite get to where he wanted to get, but he said he wants to practise more, but I'm not sure if we're going to let him practise tonight. He's having a rest. (A: He'll need a rest.) He's having a rest. (A: That's good.)

YM: All right, all right. But he said he's... mmm. All right, I'll tell them! He's saying, will you tell everybody that he's sorry he didn't say goodbye properly, (A: I know.) because he always wanted to say goodbye properly, but it was very quick and very convenient. – Not so convenient for you, but he had a good laugh about it. (A: I bet he did.) He's a little bit upset because he's a very – Yes, I know you are! He's a very strict man. – Don't tell me off. All right, cos I'm not telling you exactly what he's saying, but it's very difficult I keep telling him. (A: Yes we know.) But he's all right. (A: That's good.) He's all right. But he said he's going to go... All right, all right. What is it about that cat? (A: Charlie Brown?) I don't like cats. I've told him that, but he says he likes cats.

Ann *(laughing):* Well, some cats!

YM: I know, but I'd give it a good kick, I would. Anyway I can't talk with him much. He's got to go and sit down and watch what's happening, all right?"

*Before he left, having spoken to all the others, the young man said:* That Thomas, you know one day, you are going to see him (A: Yes.) not on the other side, on this side. You know that, but he's not quite sure who he's going to use yet, but it could take two to three years. Don't rush it 'cos you know everybody likes that old boy even though he's a bit of a miserable old g.. . He doesn't like me saying that cos he says it's disrespectful. – I know it's disrespectful, but you've got to learn as well, kid. I've told him, all right!? But he's very good 'cos he's having a good laugh now. Don't worry about it. Anyway we will see what happens.

The sitting continued for another hour with many connections for them, from their family and spirit companions. A wonderful night. What a beautiful gift to be given – to be able to speak with Tom in this way. Thank you, dear friends!

*November 9th 2010:*

This is a report published in *Spirit of PN* on the internet.

### All tied up...

Sue Farrow on an exceedingly clever communication from the late Tom Harrison:

It's not often that spirit messages come all tied up in neat little packages, but it seems that's exactly what Tom Harrison managed to do just two-and-a-half weeks after his passing on October 23.

As medium Michael Bagan lay fast asleep on the night of November 8/9th, he became aware of Tom standing by his bed. Michael and Tom had met only once, about six months ago, but that was enough for Michael to know the identity of his nocturnal visitor.

'He was smartly dressed in a suit,' said Michael 'and wearing a strange black tie. It was really narrow, not pointed at the bottom like ties normally are, it was square.'

Tom proceeded to give Michael a good deal of further evidence, some of it very detailed indeed, but Michael couldn't understand why Tom kept on pointing to the tie he was wearing.

Still puzzled by Tom's reasons for making such a big deal of the tie he was wearing, Michael, a London cabbie, set off for work in his taxi. A few hours later his mobile phone rang. It was another taxi driver, who knew that Michael sometimes went to churches and wore a suit. Someone had left a package in the back of his cab, he said, and he wondered if the tie it contained might be of any use to Michael.

'I went all hot and cold,' said Michael. 'I asked him what colour it was, and when he said 'black' I was stunned.' They arranged to meet in an hour so that Michael could have the tie. Opening the package, he was a whole lot more stunned when he saw that the tie it contained was not only black, it was also very narrow and square at the bottom.

'It was unreal,' Michael told me. 'The hairs stood up on the back of my neck. I couldn't believe it.'

Tom's wife Ann was delighted to hear the tale of the tie and the taxi drivers. She told me:

'Tom had a good collection of ties including a black one for funerals, but nothing like the one described and given to Michael. To show him something which had not entered Michael's life or mine was Tom's way of showing him it was not just a dream. The other pieces of evidence were accurate and very pertinent to me, and gave me a lift when I was about to start on the long journey back to our home in Spain, but this is particularly good for Michael and his mediumship.'

Those who knew Tom in this life will not be in the least surprised that he should have managed such an ingeniously evidential communication so soon after arriving in the spiritworld. He was a stickler for the highest and best in evidence while he was here, and it seems he hasn't changed a bit.

An interesting slant on the development of this connection is that Sue knows Michael and his mediumship well. She looked on Tom as one of her 'wise men', often seeking his advice on matters spiritual, and Tom's only meeting with Michael had been in her office just six months before. So this was a special connection through her.

*Michael Bagan*

Michael rang Sue on the Tuesday morning to tell her what had happened in his 'vision' and to pass on the personal details Tom had communicated to him.

Later that day, she caught the train to High Wycombe where I met her. She had offered to accompany me, and share the driving on the return to Spain the following day. At 5 o'clock that afternoon, as she was going through the list with me of items Michael had seen and heard from Tom, her mobile phone rang. It was Michael telling her of the receipt of the tie. You can imagine the excitement we all felt.

For me, some of the most positive evidence from this connection was the following:

Michael said, as he was waking, he saw Tom's face, right close to his own, and it startled him. He told Sue that Tom was standing by the side of the bed, holding a cup of tea which he kept giving to Michael. He could see that Tom then also held a silver 'something' in his hand, which may have been a tankard but Michael was not sure. Tom used to wake me with a cup of tea *every morning.* He was always up around 5.30 to 6am and would work on the computer until around 7.15am. (I refused to wake up before that). He would then bring me half-a-beaker of tea as he couldn't safely carry more without spilling it.

Early in that last year, we had found insulated beakers in a '99p shop' which would keep the tea hot. Tom would make the other half of the beaker of tea in the insulated beaker. As by then, he could not carry the small tray with two cups, after bringing the first one through to the bedroom, he would go back and bring the second beaker, so I could have a 'top up'. We would then snuggle down and I would enjoy a slow start to the day.

You may wonder why I let him do this every morning. It was because he was still fiercely independent and so deeply loving he needed to do this for me, and you do not take that away from anyone.

Michael also heard the name of Evan or Evans, and then heard Tom say 'I have met the person, Evans.'

When I heard the name I knew it was familiar, but it wasn't until I was able to check Tom's book that I could be sure if I was right. Sydney Shipman was a member of the Harrison home circle back in the 1940s and his guide was Rev John Evans, a Methodist preacher. He once materialised in the Saturday Night Club circle. Sydney had a small painting of him, but I have been unable to find it among the papers Gladys gave us. I'm sure this is what he was indicating, as he would now be meeting guides as well as all the old friends.

Finally, Michael told Sue that Tom plans to come through many, many mediums, but not necessarily while Ann is sitting with them. She will be told about them in phone calls.

This has certainly happened many times though not as many phone calls as emails.

Trivia!!

Yes, but meaningful 'trivia' — memories for me and connections in advance of the moment, both for the mediums and for me.

As the quotation, from Sir Oliver Lodge's book *The Reality of a Spiritual World* states:

> Who is to say what significance may not attach to trifles when properly studied and understood? A finger print is a trifle – a dirty smudge not worthy of notice – but it is no trifle to the criminal when submitted to expert scrutiny.

To close this chapter here are a few of the lovely responses to this report in *Spirit of PN*:

Terry Gardener wrote 10/12/2010 at 10:05 pm

> This is absolutely brilliant news! A tireless worker for Spirit all his physical life.... Still doing it on the other side!

Janey wrote 11/12/2010 at 12:49 am

> How fantastic is that! What a brilliant way to show you are there!

Frank Brown wrote 23/12/2010 at 12:47 pm

> Fabulous, I met Tom a couple of times and attended one of his lectures.
>
> He was a great ambassador for spirit when alive and looks like he is carrying on now he has passed.

*Seven*

# The voice verified

A week later on the 16th November, Tom made his first attempt at speaking through Stewart Alexander – an evening particularly chosen by the spirit team because Chris Eldon Lee, the Radio programme producer was present.

As Katie Halliwell wrote in her tribute to Tom in *Part 3* of her trilogy E*xperiences of Trance, Physical Mediumship and Associated Phenomena*:

> The most astonishing event of the seminar (29-31st October 2010) that weekend was to be a wonderful communication at the séance held on the Saturday evening. Ernie spoke to his wife Rose through Stewart in trance until his emotions beat him, and then Sunrise communicated through the trumpet. Many of the new guests in the séance room were not fully aware of who Sunrise was and therefore did not appreciate the value of his specific communication. To the accompaniment of communal singing, the trumpet soared around the room, finally stopping as close as it could get to Ann. Hearing breathing sounds through the trumpet Ann called to everyone to stop singing. After his special 'clearing' sound known so well to Tom and Ann and a limited number of people, Sunrise spoke – 'Sunrise greet little sister. ... All send greetings to you, with love... All is well.' – a so very reassuring message.

And so very special to me. Those closing words – 'All is well' – are the final words from a favourite piece of Tom's and mine, Canon Scott Holland's, *Death is nothing at all*, with which Tom began the Preface to his own book.

Katie continues:

> Then only 2 weeks after the seminar, Tom was able to speak for several minutes to the home circle, through Stewart's trance state. A little thing like death is not going to stop him communicating.

### Tom's return at Stewart's home circle, 16th Nov 2010

A very breathy voice was heard trying to speak.

Chris Eldon Lee (CEL): Good Evening.

Ray: Hello, my friend. (*A breathy sound again*) Nice to have you with us. Come on, you can do it. (the breathing again) You're most welcome here you know. You're most welcome.

Voice: Fir.. firs.. first try. (*but most indistinctly*)

Lindsey: Fred says Hi?

Voice: No.

June: No.

V: First.. tryv...tryv... Ohh! (*exasperated*).

J: Clive, no?

V: No.

J: No-no-no-no.

V: June.

L: June?

J: Yes?

V: No no. ... Don'...guess ... Don't ... guess. Ohh (*sighing*) (but it sounds like 'June guess')

J: No. It's difficult, come on. / CEL. Come on, come on you can do it.

L: It sounds like don't forget.

V: No, don't guess.

J: I've got to guess.

V: No, no, no ...don't guess.

J: Don't guess. We haven't to guess. (*laughter by the circle sitters, all speaking together*) / L: All right, sorry. We won't guess. / J: We've not to guess. / R: We'll leave it with you. / J: We'll leave it with you, darling. We've not to guess. /R: Come on. You're welcome anyway.

CEL: We understand.

V: ...don't...know...if...I...can...say...just...a...few... words. (*then a long breath*)

L (*repeating*): You don't know if you can say...?

V: A few ... words. / June & Chris: ... a few words.

L: You're doing well though. / CEL: We'd love to hear your words.

J: We'd like to hear you.

V: Me...me (J: You... me?) (*a heavy breath then...*) Tom.

J: Tom?

L: (*excitedly*) Yes, Tom. Is it you? J: Tom, Tom.

V: Tom: Yes.

L: Tom, you are doing fantastic / J: Love you to bits, Tom. Come on, Tom.

Tom: Really ... trying.

(*Speaking together*) L: Oh you are doing great. /J: Oh, Tom, it is wonderful./ L: Thank you for coming./ J: This is wonderful.

Tom: Just thought it time... (L: You thought it was time.) for me to come.

R: It's been too long. / J: That's wonderful. / L: Oh, Wonderful. Oh, thank you for coming and you've done ever so well./ R: You have.

CEL: We had a great celebration for you.

Tom: Aye, I know.

J: He knows. (*laughter from the circle*)

Tom: Wonderful, ... wonderful.

L: Are you enjoying yourself over there?

Tom: Wonderful ... wonderful.

J: Ahh, that's wonderful, Tom.

Tom: Tell... Ann... just had to come....I just had to come.

J: You just had to come.

CEL: You did indeed ... (L: Thank you so much.) What kept you? / J: We love you, Tom.

Tom: If I could have come sooner...( J: You would.) Yes.

J: If he could have come sooner he would have.

Tom: Give Ann my love.

J: We will give Ann your love.

Tom: Thank you.

J: You're welcome, Tom. We love you to bits, Tom.

Tom: Chris ... Chris.

L: Chris.

CEL: It's lovely to hear your voice, Tom and don't forget that if it hadn't been for you, I wouldn't be here at all.

Tom: Yes, (*speaking much more rapidly now*) but what... what is important now, is that you are here and everything I said about it, it is all that and more.

L: Brilliant. (*with comments on top of each other from the others too*)

CEL: Absolutely.

Tom: God bless.

All: God bless, Tom./ Love you to bits, Tom. / Thank you.

J: He grabbed my hand as he... L: He tried to take mine.

CEL: Is that the first time that Tom...?

J: That he's been through here, Yes.

CEL: ...spoken?      June: In here, yes.

There is a creaking sound and Walter takes over control.

J: Hello, Walter.

Walter: Now, folks, that was a surprise.

L: That was really nice surprise / J: It was a wonderful surprise.

L: He did fantastic as well.

Walter: Well let me say that he was most insistent.

J: Ohh, was he.

CEL: Funny you should say that.

L: Give him our love.

W: Of course, he has such a will.

J: He has and always will have.

W: You would expect nothing less.

J: No, no, definitely not.

W: OK, so we thought that the time was opportune, particularly since our friend Chris... (CEL: Hello, Walter.)

J: ... was here, yes.

CEL: That's very kind, Walter.

W: You were able to hear him?

J: Yes, yes we were.

CEL: I was looking at his photograph on the wall downstairs just a few minutes ago (*see photo opposite*)

W: Yes. He is insistent that his wife, Ann, is informed.

J: Ray will tell her, won't you Ray.

R: Yes I will.

J: Ray will let her know.

Walter: OK, OK, ...

This is what Chris Eldon Lee wrote to me after the sitting:

As you will almost certainly know by now, Tom made a remarkable entrance at Hull on Tuesday. He chose a select audience, with just the five of us there – Ray, June, Lindsey, Stewart and a very privileged me. Funnily enough my eyes had been drawn to study the wedding photo on Ray's wall, in which Tom stands so strong and statuesque. So it didn't come as a complete surprise.

His was the first voice to be heard and he came through almost at once, indistinctly at first calling 'June, June' and then more clearly. He told us off for trying to guess who he was before he'd had chance to introduce himself. But his voice gave him away. It sounded just like Tom*. It could not possibly have been anyone else. ...

I must say that for the very first time in circle, the hairs on the back of my neck stood up and tingled and tingled whilst he was present. It was a very powerful and moving feeling and I was so very glad to be present.

\* And Chris should know the sound of Tom's voice as he spent many hours listening to it when producing the BBC Radio 4 Broadcast *Christmas Spirits* in 2003.

*Tom performing a blessing ceremony at the marriage of Chris and Hannah in May 2009*

*Eight*

# Eric's connection with Tom

In October, Eric and Jackie were on holiday in Madeira when we arrived back in Yorkshire, so we did not see them on Tom's final trip home. One month later, when Eric was in a great deal of pain with torn tendons in his shoulder, he wrote of the experience he had that evening:

*November 25th, 2010:*

I had such a spiritual experience last night that I am writing it down so that I don't forget it.

First, I need to go back to the night before my operation, ten days ago. I often use Tom's protection prayer before opening my mind to all good spirits. That night nearly all the spirits I have ever seen in these situations, popped in to give me energy for the following day. They included Bill, Phillip, all my uncles, Doug, Auntie Florrie, Chris and many more. The ones missing were Tom, the 'Bish', my mam and Jackie's mum. There was, however, a new spirit, Julia, the wife of a colleague, and she was so strong that she seemed to take charge of the event.

Julia died on 20th February of this year and although I have felt her presence, this was the first time I 'saw' her. She was always a strong lady, had psychic senses and was someone I had hypnotised on a number of occasions. So to last night – I was in bed and couldn't get to sleep. I opened my mind to friendly spirits – nothing for ages and then I was aware of an urge to recite my Chinaman joke and since it was Tom's favourite, I did.

Briefly:

| | |
|---|---|
| Bin man to Chinaman | 'Where's your bin?' |
| Chinaman | 'I's bin to China' |
| Bin man | 'No where's your dustbin?' |
| Chinaman | 'I dust bin to China' |
| Bin man | 'No! Where's your wheelie dustbin?' |
| Chinaman | 'I weelie dust bin to China' |

Immediately I saw Tom – top right corner of my mind's eye, laughing and saying 'Yer daft beggar' and 'Thanks, Son,' as he always called me. Then everything went mad with all my spirit friends popping in and Tom insisting that I introduce them to him. The exceptions were the same as before. There was a real party atmosphere.

Everything was almost finished when I was suddenly aware of Julia saying that I hadn't introduced her to Tom. I then had to try and get Tom back, which was remarkably easy and then introduced them. They seemed to have a long chat and both were smiling.

I was quite exhausted at the end of it and it is one of the strongest I have experienced. Needless to say, I couldn't get to sleep and am writing this at 2am.

Eric is not a spiritualist and only knows what he does from Tom, who told Eric that he had an awareness of spirit and should develop it. It seems that is what has happened.

I must explain 'the 'Bish' – is Jackie's godfather, once Bishop of Sheffield, who officiated at their wedding, so that Jackie's father, who was a vicar, could give her away. Tom was often aware of both the 'Bish' and Jackie's father working with him when we were doing healing work, particularly when working with Eric. Sometimes the connection with them was apparent when Tom made characteristic hand movements, known to Eric but not to us. So it was good to have the churchmen working alongside us.

How did this strong connection and wonderful friendship with Eric and Jackie come about?

In 1996, through two friends in the Spiritualist movement Tom was put forward for induction into the Freemasons. These two friends mentioned it to him quite independently, 190 miles apart and unbeknown to each other, although they were both in the same Lodge in York, and he accepted their invitation. He had considered it for many years but because of the expense involved he had been advised not to go into the movement when younger with a growing family.

In 1997, Eric was having problems with his knee, having fallen downstairs, and Marjorie, another friend of ours, during a masonic social evening, advised him to come and see us for healing. Instead of healing for himself, he brought a terminally ill friend. The team in the spirit world could not cure him – that was not in their, or our, remit. When he arrived, he was hardly able to walk into the house. After we had asked the Divine Spirit and our healing team for help, he was able to walk down the winding path to the car, with a definite spring in his step, and we were able to let him have an easier transition to the spirit world.

When, some months later, we did finally work with Eric, Tom was aware of Eric's family members who had passed. This developed a strong bond between them, and Eric wrote a section for Tom's book *Life After Death: Living Proof*, about his special experience in our own home circle only two days before his second major heart operation. After this operation, we were called in by Jackie to give healing energy when Eric developed pleurisy – a big step to take for this vicar's daughter.

Later, when Tom's book was in print, Eric volunteered to be in charge of posting the orders.

We spent many hours together, and Eric and Jackie also visited us in Spain. One year they stayed in our home in

Spain while we toured England. One of their most memorable visits was when they flew over to Spain for Tom's Spanish ninetieth birthday party. He had no idea that they were coming so it was a wonderful surprise for him.

*Eric and Jackie with Tom during their visit to Spain in 2000*

Eric always joined in our distant healing sessions on a Thursday morning, and so close was the link that we occasionally were able to pick up any problem he had and could report it back to him.

When we planted the tree in memory of Tom at Cober Hill at the beginning of April 2011 Jackie had been suffering with endometrial cancer for many months but was responding well to treatment. She looked extremely well and came to a séance with Stewart Alexander the following evening, when Tom and her father came and spoke to her. Later in the sitting, Dr Barnett materialised to give her some healing, and told her to think of him each night as she went to bed so he could attend to continue the process.

Jackie passed quietly into spirit just two months later, and only seven-and-half months after Tom. The previous August, when we had been doing some distant healing work for Jackie, Tom had been impressed to tell her: "In ten months you'll be fine!"

Jackie set great store by the things Tom said, so a few days before she died she commented to Eric "Well, Tom got that wrong, didn't he!" Eric replied "Well no, he didn't. You will be fine, but not in the way we thought it would be."

In mid-June I returned to England for Jackie's funeral and took the opportunity of sitting again with the Hull Circle the following evening.

Eric had asked me to ask Tom if he had organised a party for Jackie when she had joined them. This I duly did and received this reply:

> Tom: Tell Eric we've got her safe. She's here. Oh! She's here. What a wonderful reunion. Make sure that he knows all is fine. (Ann: I will.) All is well.
>
> A: He wants to know if you've been organising a party for her.
>
> Tom: Well, I think you know the answer to that. Yes, yes. (A: I thought you would have.) What a wonderful, wonderful, wonderful time we have all had here since she came over. (A: That's great.)

Following Jackie's death Eric had a very difficult year but he wrote this to me in March 2012.

> I am still awake thanks to Tom and it is 12.55am!
>
> I went to bed after the news, did the crossword and couldn't get to sleep. I said Tom's protection prayer and then asked for healing from Dr Barnett as I often do.

I was then aware of Tom. So I asked him if he has met Jackie and he gave a beaming smile, and I was aware of him walking through the market you took us to (in Spain), where he bought a bag of cherries. He was giving some to Jackie. She was smiling.

It was so strong and so unexpected that I got up and went down into the lounge where Tom always thought there was a lot of energy. There was more of the same but Jackie wasn't as strong as Tom; it was almost as though he was helping her. Then came the flood of friends and relations all trying to get in – as you know this used to happen to me a lot, but not for about 18 months.

After that, I came down to the office and opened the computer. There was Gill's email, which had taken a few hours to come through. I believe that was Jackie *et al.* saying congratulations to Gill.

Hopefully, I will be able to sleep now, but I had to write this down while it was fresh in my memory.


The email from their daughter Gill, then an engineer in the oil industry, was to tell him that she had been promoted to business manager of the company she worked in.

A month later, I was due to take Eric and Gill to sit in Stewart's home circle but unfortunately, Eric was taken ill that afternoon. However it was a special evening for Gill as she was able to speak to her mother and to her maternal grandfather, and later I was able to sit beside Stewart and speak with Tom.

Such special, close, loving occasions.

*Nine*

# Where next?

Around the same time in November 2010, as Eric had those experiences in York, I went to the regular Sunday service at the Acacia Centre in Spain, just four weeks after Tom had left the physical state. He didn't believe in staying away from there either.

Morag, the medium for that morning, lives locally and is well known to us all at the centre but on a personal level she knows little about us. Following a few opening statements, which I accepted as understood, she stated "There is an anniversary in May and they are giving you a red rose." She stopped suddenly and gasped as she felt Tom's energy draw close, quite forcefully. – "Yes," I replied "May is our wedding anniversary." My tears started to flow.

She continued "He's saying there have been too many tears – you know how it works!"

My goodness, I was getting a scolding from the spirit world!

But yes, I do know how it works.

When you are weeping and full of sorrow, it is distressing for them as they feel your grief, and it is as though there is a thick 'mist' around you that they cannot penetrate. Tom tells the story in his book of a spirit child they helped, back in 1948. Young James Andrew had found that when he tried to return to his home in Haverton Hill he couldn't get through the mist around it. Attracted by the bright spiritual light, shining from the Saturday Night Club circle, he spoke to them through the trumpet 'megaphone'. Tom later called on the parents and was able to explain to them how their son had wanted to make himself known. Their lives were changed by knowing that their son still lived and he was able to get back to be with them when he wanted to.

Being a spiritualist or survivalist may take away the deep sorrow of feeling that you are parted for ever. Nevertheless, it still takes time to get through the grief of not having that physical presence to hold, to kiss, to care for. I'm not sufficiently tuned in, to get instant answers to the questions I ask. Mind you, I probably would think it was just me thinking up the answer so it is better for it to come through someone else who didn't know I'd even asked a question.

Dr Annette Childs summed up an article she wrote titled *'Got Grief?'* in this way:

> Regardless of what one's afterlife knowledge may be, grief is grief. The universality of the experience of grief can perhaps be best summed-up by the statement once made by Edwin Shneidman, founder of the Suicide Prevention Center in Los Angeles. He says 'Grief is the ransom you pay for love.' Indeed, whether one is a world-renowned afterlife researcher or simply the bereft neighbour of one gone too soon, this bandit of grief finds its way into the most carefully locked fortresses among us. May we be gentle and far-seeing with one another and as individuals allow grief its rightful passage when it is our ransom to pay.

As Morag completed her communication from Tom, she turned to Robert, saying "He wasn't asleep in the circle – he knew everything that was going on – he was in an altered state!"

This statement certainly lightened the morning's proceedings, causing the home circle members to laugh heartily. For there had been times when Tom had been asleep during our dark sittings, particularly the one when he woke and said "Who's turned my light out?"

He had woken, thinking he was at home in bed, and the low-wattage bedside lamp, which was lit throughout the night, had been turned off! – Happy memories for us all.

Morag's reading for the service that morning gave us a further connection. It was not her usual philosophy from Silver Birch but '*The Canadian 5-cent piece*' from Tom's own book. When working closely with spirit, we try to allow ourselves to be guided in our choice of reading for a Sunday service, being 'drawn' to a particular book or poem, to fit in with whatever will be spirit's theme for the day. She wasn't to know when she chose it that she would be working with Tom again that morning.

Tom never missed a chance to make himself known at the centre, and two weeks later Gay Nash, having established a contact with Rob and Barbara went on to say "Thomas will always be here. He knows of the arrangements and the merriment, and it is all really starting in the New Year. With him is a little girl with dark hair who has got prettier." – (that would be his granddaughter Susan who died in 1981.)

The arrangements were for the physical mediumship events which had been planned for the following August, with physical medium David Thompson, and then in the November, Scott Milligan was to be with us. Tom wasn't being left out of those!

Following that initial breakthrough, working with clairaudient, clairsentient and clairvoyant mediums, with two different trance mediums and a friend who would not profess to be any sort of medium, I began to realise that I could expect him to try anything.

In early December, with the onset of Christmas tidings to friends whom I had not previously contacted, Ray, a long-time medium friend, now also in Spain, wrote:

"In mid-November when Tom came to me, it was early morning as I was getting ready to go out. He was 'content', and just said, 'I'm on the other side, a bit of a surprise, but I'm OK! You will be hearing more from Ann'."

Then just before Christmas when I was at last able to contact Kate, she replied:

"I know you will believe me when I say that around bonfire night (November 5th), our circle began to pick up the name TOM and I could see him smiling. I said at that time, Tom is either very ill or he may have passed. Now we have proof that he has 'gone home'."

* * * * *

Three months later, in early March, Kate and two members of her circle came for a week's holiday in nearby Torrevieja and we spent a lot of time together. When I was showing them around our home for the first time, Tom drew so close to Kate that she felt a sharp pain in the back of her head and became dizzy. She had picked up one of his last sensations on earth – the blow to the back of his head. How well I got to know that feeling myself – a good indication that he was near, until he learned to overcome it.

When Tom interrupts the emails she is writing to pass on messages to me she is very aware of him beside her. She stresses she hears his voice – "just as I remembered with that slight accent."

Among many other things he communicated through her that afternoon in our home, was the news that there was a special occasion coming up; he would have his best bib and tucker on and I would feel him hold my hand.

In March, I also heard that he had been recognised, mentally, by some members in the home circle of our friend Anne in South Wales. There was also contact in northern Spain, but that deserves a chapter to itself.

When the Hull circle started sitting again after a winter break, Tom was quickly there at the beginning of the evening. In his distinctive voice, he spoke quietly for several minutes. He said that it was like old times, except now he could speak when he liked. He was surprised how difficult it was – far more difficult than he had imagined. When Lindsey, Stewart's niece, said "Is it a bit of a struggle?" he replied that that was something of an understatement! He then continued:

> "I think if I continue to try I should become quite good at this. I had such a surprise when I came over here. So many people to greet me, so many people waiting for me to come. It surpassed my wildest dreams.
>
> At this point, June said: "It's Tom isn't it?"
>
> "Yes, don't worry if you can't recognise my voice but it is so difficult doing this," Lindsey commented that she thought he was doing brilliantly to which he replied "Well let's face it, I've been preparing for many years."

He then sent his love to me, and asked me to pass on his love to all his friends, and tell them that he had been to Stewart's circle. He was unable to say much more then, but promising to get stronger, he passed on a message from Stewart's sister, Gaynor to Lindsey, her daughter. He went on to say how his illness had been gradually defeating him, but now he was free of it all and he was well. On leaving, he stressed how he still loved them all, in just the same way as he always had, and thanked them for allowing him to be part of their lives. He had spoken constantly, and clearly, for five minutes – some feat this early in his progress.

Only three weeks after their trip to Spain, on the 1st April, I was able to sit with Kate's circle in the northwest of England, during my Spring-time trip to UK. It was good to meet up again with old friends from the spirit world, particularly with Clarence, a clown whose face I had first seen through Kate's transfiguration in 1998 at our home near Selby.

But before Clarence came through at the end of the circle, after an hour of sitting we had this surprise.

> Kathleen, (one of the sitters): And I don't know why, Ann, but I've got to give you some cinder toffee.
> Ann: Ah, yes.
> Kate: Just to prove they are here.
> Ann: Yes, that's Mam.

Kate and I were both aware that Tom's 'old family circle' were there and had heard 'The gang's all here'. With that, Kate went back into trance, and Raven came and asked for a dim light. After a few minutes a spirit friend I felt I recognised was there to assist Tom. At first, Tom struggled to show himself and just managed to tell me how he missed me.

He kept working at the control and a few minutes later he managed to say it was hard but he was trying. Then, at first haltingly, we heard a few words:

> Tom: The face here. Tom-Tom: Not for the faint hearted.
> Ann: You need to have more energy drawn from the sitters to help you.
> Tom: Energy will grow down from the neck and get bigger and bigger and a ball will turn into a ........
> Ann: I just want to confirm you will be drawing energy from the sitters as well to help you.
> Tom: Imperative!
> Ann: So you'll need us to keep fairly still while this is being done.
> Tom: Imperative!

Ann: Yes. Understand.

Tom: If you were close enough you would feel the electricity.

G: We can see it, Tom.

Tom: Like my Mam's.

Ann: Yes, good.

Tom: This is Mam's team. They'll help and I'll help. Now we've built the bridge. You know what I mean, love. I do love you.

Ann: I do indeed, I do indeed. (*He was referring to the painting which he could not complete until Doris passed when he could join the two sides*).

T: And I do love you. (A: I love you too.) And it's so....! I tried to be strong.

A: You did, you were.

T: Ann, these are my hands, they're not Kate's.

Ann: I can see. I can see the base of that thumb and its enlarged joint.

T: They're mine they're mine and I'm sat in this chair and I'm with you, my love. I'm here. And Kate, Oh thank you, thank you! Not just a voice, my love. I'm here, my feet, my legs. Ohh! Wonderful. In Spain a voice – part Tom but this is all Tom. (*referring to the sitting with Kate there* )

A: Well done, Darling. Yes I can see that thumb joint.

T: I can see you! Are you able to see my eyes?

A: Yes. / Greta: Yes.

T: I'm trying so hard. Can you see my eyes? I can see you. You are so beautiful because I can see your energy.

Ann: Thank you.

Tom: Thank you, my new friends.

G: You're very welcome, Tom.

T: Thank you, my old friend. Thank her so much. (*meaning Kate*)    (A: We will do. / G: We'll tell her.)

T: I'm not going yet because I've an excuse. I'm working you see.

A: You are, not just popped in.

T: By the way – Ching Lee. It was Ching Lee.

A: I waited for him to do his hand movements and he didn't.

T: No, because I had to do mine.

A: I thought that if you were coming that was who it would likely be but he didn't put his arms together.

T: Sly goat! *(laughter)* Still transforming ...possibly. See the light? Now, my dear, put your hand between my hands. Not touch but can you feel?

A: Ooo yes, tingling in my finger ends.

T: Isn't this magic? *(the voice becomes lighter in tone)*

A: It is magic. Brilliant! It's like pinpricks all through.

T: That's right – electricity.

A: Back of my hand now.

T: That's right ... Better than Paul Daniels!

A *(chuckling)*: Far better than Paul Daniels.

T: Eat your heart out! Isn't this something? And my new friend, do likewise. You must feel this is what you are working with.

Greta: Oh my god!

T: Isn't that something?

G: That is. Very strong.

T: *(to Marie)* My lady as well. In between, my dear. You got it? Isn't that marvellous? Thank you. This is what you are working towards; building the energy ball towards – so that we can bring our faces to push.

G: That would be marvellous. Thank you so much. Bless you.....It's food for spirit.

A: You have done so well.

T: You know when I go. I won't go. *(the voice changes back to more like Tom's)*

A: I know.

T: I brought you here, my love.

A: You did.

T: We'll meet soon. Watch what I do.

A: Salutes!

T: Now we can touch to say goodbye. Take me with you and I take you with me. One last look.

I reached out and touched his outstretched hand and the energy faded.

After another communicator, who brought a lot of energy with him, Clarence came to close the circle, and this is what he had to say about the excess weight in my car on that trip and Tom's reception on arrival in the spirit world.

> Clarence: I've been pumping your tyres up. (Ann: Good, thank you.) Yes, it needed it. In fact I nearly had to get jack out. I thought my goodness what she got in here. You see I've met Tom. He's been trying my boots on. They nearly fit him. He's a good laugh.
>
> Ann: He is.
>
> Cl: Ooo yeah! Yeah, I were there, I were in queue. I thought I know this guy. I'll make him at home. Ooo, the amount of folks up there – Good grief. Well, if I'd had a ball we could have had a game of football, 'cos filled the stadium it did – He's a good man.

In mid-April, I visited Alf and June Winchester in Norfolk, following the tree planting in Tom's memory, at Cober Hill. Whilst giving me healing, Alf became aware of Tom kneeling in front of me – as Alf said, not 'proposing' to me but giving healing. He saw Tom dressed in a pale blue Pringle-type pullover, but without a logo. As he thought about it, a logo appeared, of two mountains with a line across them. This, I later realised, was the description of the logo of our local hospital in Spain, where Tom had been a patient. The mountains are in fact heaps of salt, dredged from the salt lake and this was the view I had from Tom's hospital room when he was a patient there with pneumonia, in 2007.

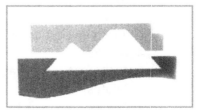

*Torrevieja Hospital logo*

By using this symbol, he was showing that he was at work – healing – cryptically using a symbol only I would understand. Even the colours of his pullover and slacks, pale blue and cream, were the colours of the clothes he preferred, when working outside.

*Tom at work!*
*Pressure washing the court-*
*yard after the winter.*
*I'm sorry, I can't show you*
*the colours of his clothes but*
*they were a pale blue jumper*
*and cream (paint-splashed)*
*trousers.*

In May, Doreen in Northumberland, a lovely friend, a medium and devoted worker for spirit, whom we knew from their time here in Spain, told me she had twice been aware of Tom saying that they were doing all they could to help with her cancer. For her though, a long life here was not to be and she passed thirteen months later.

At the Hull circle, towards the end of May, when Katie Halliwell told Tom she would tell me that he had been to the guest circle, he informed them, through Stewart's trance, "She's sunning herself." I had, indeed, flown off that day to Ibiza, for a week at Hans Schaer's *Finca* in Ibiza, to enjoy the company of Kai Mügge's Felix circle with a number of other guests, where I had a chance to relax and unwind in the presence of old and new friends.

By now it wasn't only Tom who was making his presence known. At the end of May, Kate (Maesen) became aware of

Tom's aunt, Mrs Abbott working with her when giving clairaudient messages. More usually known to us and many as Aunt Agg, she was an accomplished trance and demonstrating medium in London in the 1930s. It then appeared that the whole of Tom's old home circle were working with Kate's circle. Kate wrote:

> Last night we had our Friday Circle (all were present) and halfway through, strong features of a North American Indian built. His voice was deep as he pronounced his name – 'Sunrise' – which echoed around the room. He said he had brought his circle with him. He was holding my left hand and he brought what the sitters saw (at first) an orange flame – then they saw it was an orange feather. My right hand was being held by Tom and for a few minutes they took it in turns to fade in and out – showing their different faces. Tom said he was looking after you and sent his love to everyone.
>
> I thought the feather was truly amazing and how blessed are we to be part of such wonderful work and proof.

Although Kate is in a fairly deep trance, and knows nothing of what is said, she is aware which spirits are close. If they are directing her movements or speaking, she feels them take her hands as a method of control.

Kate is mainly a transfiguration medium and the faces develop over hers. Sunrise was Tom's mother's guide and 'doorkeeper' or protector of the circle, but Sunrise has continued to be a close friend to Tom all his life and now also returns to me.

None of those in the circle, apart from Kate, knew of the events on the first Anniversary of the old circle in 1947. When, after Sunrise had materialised in full head-dress, Tom's Aunt Agg had materialised and, on Sunrise's behalf, brought an orange feather as an apport. This feather is still in Tom's memorabilia. Sunrise had wanted to bring them a feather from his own head-dress, but after three hundred years it no longer existed.

*Tom's Aunt Agg, as she materialised in red light in their circle in February 1948 (22 months after they started sitting). Minnie is behind the black curtain. The man (left) is Tom's father, who moved during the two minute exposure. This photograph was taken by Agnes' son, Terry.*

\* \* \* \* \*

How busy Tom has been in this first seven months! Some mediums say you must wait six months before you go for a sitting. Tom couldn't wait to come and contact us.

This swift return has happened many times, to many people throughout the years, particularly when there is a good knowledge of our survival after physical death.

I remember Geoff Everatt telling us of one such occurrence, on his first visit to see Helen Duncan, in 1938. During the evening there were a number of materialisations, and one of them had a long conversation with the people in front of Geoff. After the séance had finished, Geoff asked them if they knew the man who had come. Their reply astonished him. It was their father, whose body was still at home in the coffin as they had not yet been able to have the funeral.

They obviously had firm knowledge of survival, but this next account of a prompt return was when there was no knowledge but a great need. In her book *While I Remember* Ivy Northage tells of a public demonstration of clairvoyance in London, by Estelle Roberts.

While Ivy and her mother were queueing to get in to the room booked for the evening, a woman joined them and asked if they had been before to something like this before. She was very worried that she was about to do something very wicked. She then told them that her brother, a vicar, had just died, and she burst into tears.

"I'm so ashamed," she said "here I am, the sister of a vicar. I have supported him all these years and now that he has died, I have no belief, no comfort. I have nothing I can hold on to, and I am so ashamed. If only he could tell me that he is still around somewhere! Then I feel I could face life without him."

He had only suffered a brief illness and it was still the custom then to bring the dead home. The night before he was to be buried she had entered the room where his coffin was placed in the centre. She went up to the open coffin, took hold of his hand and held it, and said "Oh, Charles, if there is anything – anything at all – that you can tell me that will assure me that you have not gone, please, please, try!"

She had then taken a rose from a vase, snapped off the stem, uncurled his fingers and placed it between his fingers and the palm of his hand, and then closed them again.

She didn't know how she had heard of the Estelle Roberts' demonstration but she had to know if there was something more.

In Estelle's demonstration, message after message was given and accepted. Then near the end, Estelle said "I want to come to the lady sitting near the back. The lady in navy with a very large hat." Ivy nudged her and told her just to answer 'Yes'.

She lifted her head and murmured assent.

"Your brother is here," announced Estelle Roberts from the platform. "He has asked me to say that he heard exactly what you were asking of him and that yes, of course he is still with you, and of course he will continue in his love and protection of you. He is telling me that you did this –." She turned and marched across the platform to a vase of flowers, took one out and snapped the stem. "You brought it back," she went on "you uncurled his hand, you placed the flower within his fingers and you put it back on his chest. He knew, he is saying 'I knew. I was there and I will always be there'."

That was the last message of the afternoon. The lady's tears after that were tears of joy.

Ivy Northage wrote, that for the very first time she realized what a wonderful gift mediumship could be, and she went on to work at her gift, becoming a wonderful medium and teacher for many years.

*Ten*

# "Here, grow a tree!"

At 2 o'clock on the afternoon of 7th April 2011, the chill wind of the morning had dropped and the sky had cleared of all cloud. In a sheltered area next to the woodland, in the extensive gardens of the Cober Hill Hotel and Conference Centre near Scarborough, twenty friends met to plant a tree in memory of their dear friend Tom.

Our auspicious meeting with Frederick and Valerie, in South Africa in 1998, led also to this other special event.

Pretoria is only an hour's drive from where Tom's eldest son, Colin, lives. As we had all day to make the journey, he decided that we would visit General Jan Smuts' house (now a museum), and the tree-filled Peace garden beside it.

In the shade of these old trees, Colin picked up an acorn and said to us "Here grow a tree!" and that became the tree we planted in Tom's memory twelve years later.

On our return from South Africa I planted that acorn in a small pot, placed it in a polythene bag, and stood it on top of the tall kitchen cupboard.

About three months later, having forgotten all about it, I noticed this bag and wondered what it was. There in the pot, straining to get out, was a three-inch-high baby oak tree. As it was now Spring, I took a chance. I moved it into a larger pot and gradually introduced it to the English weather.

It grew!

However, only one year on we were on the move and when it was about six inches high, we left it in the care of my brother in Beverley when we moved to Spain.

During each visit, as it grew and John moved it into ever larger pots, Tom would say "I wish we could find somewhere safe where the tree could grow to be tall."

*Our tree - 15 months old*

When I was trying to think of a memorial to Tom, I asked John if he would mind if I planted the tree somewhere in a wood. He was rather sorry to see it go, having cared for it for ten years and with Stewart Alexander's help, instead of just any woodland, we got permission to plant it near to Gaynor's seat at Cober Hill.

Two years earlier, a level area had been created in this sloping grassy bank, to take a commemorative seat in memory of Stewart's sister, Gaynor, tragically killed in a car crash. Now we were there to plant a tree in honour of Tom, and scatter his ashes there, to nourish the young oak tree.

I began the ceremony by reading Tom's mother's poem *The Homeward Road* – a favourite of his and used at many funerals.

Eric then took over from me, telling everyone the story of the growing of the tree, which you have just read, and sharing with us his memories of Tom, serious and funny. He told us that, despite the disparity of twenty-seven years, there seemed no age gap between them, so lively was Tom's mind.

Stewart Alexander followed Eric, adding his thoughts and then reading Bishop Brent's piece on dying:

A ship sails.

I am standing on the sea shore.
A ship sails and spreads her white sails to the morning breeze and starts for the ocean.
She is an object of beauty and I stand watching her till at last she fades on the horizon,
and someone at my side says:
'She is gone.'
Gone where? Gone from my sight, that is all;
she is just as large in the masts, hull and spars
as she was when I saw her.
The diminished size and total loss of sight is in me, not her;
and just at the moment when someone at my side says;
'She's gone'
there are others who are watching her coming
and other voices take up a glad shout,
'There she comes', — and that is dying.

As Stewart was reading this, a large white ship, far out by the horizon, sailed across the view we had of the sea from our vantage point.

I then read some short tributes to Tom which I had received in emails and cards, including these:

from Dr Hans Schaer – in Switzerland:

We all love Tom, his warm, kind and noble personality and admire his dedication to spirituality, so the fact that none of us was ever to meet Tom again, – at least on this plane, – made us all extremely sad. I am purposely not writing in the 'past-form' because we still love and appreciate Tom and will continue to do so.

from John and Clare Samson in Haywards Heath:

> Tom was a very special person – quite unique – and the oak-tree planting ceremony at Cober. How right that seems!
>
> Tom was one of the rare ones: the light just shone out of his dear face and lifted one up when one was with him – a truly beautiful soul.

and from Marjorie in York:

> Tom was a very special person and I hold his memory very dear to my heart.

I followed the tributes with these words as a form of 'committal':

> We return to the earth that which has come from the earth, from time immemorial, in the knowledge that the fine spirit it carried is free to continue on his way for all eternity. Able to draw close to us when he desires and yet also to grow in his own progression and fly.
>
> We love you, remember you and will always walk with your memory here and eventually with you hereafter.
>
> God Bless you, dearest Tom.

Earth and ashes were then added by several of us to the hole in which the tree had been placed by the gardeners and I closed with the following invocation.

*Sandy's tribute to Tom*

> Divine Spirit and Guardians of this place and its trees, we ask for your help, that this little tree, so lovingly nurtured by John, may grow strong and tall to give delight to all who come here.

We then made our way back into the house, passing the daffodils in full bloom and leaving the gardeners to finish off the planting.

Refreshments, which included Linda's delicious home-made buns, were soon consumed in the conservatory, with a number of people sitting outside in the warm sunshine.

– How Tom would have loved those cakes!

---

**The Homeward Road**

You have passed beyond our sight
 along the unseen way,
On the homeward journey
 that we all must take someday.

In heart and home you leave a gap
 that no-one else can fill.
You have gone – and yet it seems
 that you are near us still.

You are only just a step ahead,
 around the hidden bend;
On the road that leads us homeward
 to our journey's end.

Though the sorrows of bereavement
 linger in our mind,
Happy is the memory
 that you have left behind.

---

We expressed our thanks to Harry and Dan, the gardeners, and to Linda and all the staff for their usual wonderful warm welcome and care.

– Three and half years on, the tree is growing well on that sunny bank, in the peace of that beautiful place, and now two rose bushes have been added to the garden alongside the seat, in memory of dear Ernie Crone.

*October 2014.*
*The tree is now almost*
*8-feet tall. The tip is right*
*at the top of the picture.*

The following evening, I took Eric and Jackie to Stewart's home circle which had been re-arranged especially for us. And it wasn't long before Tom was speaking to us.

Tom: ... so difficult for me to speak

Ann: I think you are doing so well

T: I'm trying so hard. I just want you to know how proud I am of you. Well done!

A: Did you enjoy yesterday?

T: Oh, did I. Oh, did I, Wonderful! Do something for me.

A: Yes, my love.

T: Thank them all.

A: Yes I will.

T: Thank everyone, I was so moved by it.

A: Lovely.

T: I don't know how long I shall be able to keep this up but let me tell you something.

A: Yes?

T: I thought I knew so much about what was waiting for me – I knew nowt!

A: You knew nowt. (*laughter*) ...............

T: I've just noticed Eric and Jackie are here.

A: They are both here.

Jackie: Yes, we're here Tom./ Eric: We're here Tom.

T: I couldn't help laughing, I couldn't help laughing at what you said.

A *(laughing)*: I know what a thing to say at the scattering of ashes!

T: Just what I thought ... Very memorable, very memorable!

A: Very memorable.

T: Ann, I don't know how much I can talk but please thank everyone... Darling, you know always I'm with ... always close by, always close by. I'll be waiting for you ... not for a long, long time. Love to you all.

At the tree ceremony, the previous afternoon, Eric had recounted the occasion when, on one of our visits to them, he had taken Tom as a visitor to their Freemasons' Lodge meeting. He lent Tom a dinner-jacket and trousers, and we had managed to equip him with all the appropriate accessories of bow-tie, shoes, etc. Eric was considerably more portly than Tom, but Tom insisted that he did not need braces for the trousers (nor a belt).

During the proceedings in the Temple that evening they were required to stand, and at this point, Tom leaned towards Eric and whispered "My trousers are round my ankles." With aplomb, he reached down and pulled his trousers up. But on his other side was a visitor who had accompanied the Master of another Lodge, who was the Invited Guest for that evening. Goodness knows what he thought! Thankfully they were in the second row and it was not witnessed by many.

On their return home, Eric told us what had happened and amidst our laughter we said at least they could dine out on the story for many years! Little did we know of one occasion when the story would be re-told. It was to this that Tom referred in his communication through Stewart.

It was the first time Jackie had had courage to sit in a séance and that evening she was able to sit beside Stewart and to speak with her father, Bill. He made an enormous effort to communicate with her. Jackie told us later that all the time he was holding her hand she could feel it shaking with the tremor of the Parkinson's disease which he had at the end of his life. Freda, one of Stewart's main spirit communicators, said she also picked up the tremor, as he was standing close to her in the spirit world.

So very often when they return to this physical world our friends return with the physical ailments that they had at the end of their life. Sometimes only briefly, until they conquer them, as Tom has done with the pain of the blow to the head, so it is not surprising that Bill brought the tremor through Stewart's hand.

Dr Barnett, the spirit doctor, then came to give Jackie healing, transferring to her the energies from the spirit world, doing all he could to help her. He also told her to think of him each evening before she went to sleep so he could attend to help her with the healing energy in that way too.

Tom's voice was still quite low in volume, but clearer now he was practising speaking through Stewart fairly frequently.

I found it intriguing that he said he thought he knew quite a bit of what to expect in the Spirit world, but he knew 'nowt' – a good Yorkshire expression for 'nothing'.

*Eleven*

# Speaking Portuguese?

In June, I had a very special telephone call from my friend Anabela Cardoso in north-west Spain.

We met in 2004 at the *Conference on Research into Survival of Physical Death with Special Reference to Instrumental Transcommunication* which she had organised with David Fontana, and since 2006 at the request of David Fontana I have been production editor of her *ITC Journal.* For years, Anabela has been receiving and researching the anomalous voices which appear on tape recordings (EVP) and through radios (DRV). These are recorded for further analysis. She told me that she had had a message on a Direct Radio Voice (DRV) recording in March saying – 'Sou o Tom' – 'I am Tom'. Before telling me about it and sending me a copy of the sound file she had sent it to many Portuguese-speaking people to verify that is indeed what it said. Her account of it was published in the ITC Journal No.41, and she has given me permission to reprint it here.

## SOU O TOM!

Anabela Cardoso

On Thursday, the 31st of March 2011, during one of Rio do Tempo's customary speech practising sessions at my house that I have described elsewhere, the most unexpected voice came through. It was a loud, fast and utterly clear voice that almost shouted in Portuguese "Sou o Tom!" (I am Tom!).

This evening Rio do Tempo's contact lasted for over thirty minutes. It had started with one of the usual feminine voices that, following Friedrich Jürgenson's classification of the clearest voices I tend to attribute to the 'speakers' of Rio do Tempo. Firstly the voice announced: "Oh Bela, o Luís!" (Bela, Luís!). Bela, as most of our readers already know, is my pet name used only by very close family members and Luís was my deceased brother's name. The voices talked a lot that evening saying things like, (translation from the Portuguese): 'It's your mother', 'It's your father', 'It is the voice', 'It's the contact of Rio do Tempo' and so on. Every now and then, during these working sessions, the voices repeat sentences several times in an obvious exercise of speech, as mentioned by other transcommunicators, (e.g. Alvisi, Schäfer amongst others).

The powerful masculine voice said "Sou o Tom!" at 0,0dB, my audio software's top measurement. It was immediately followed by one of the clear feminine voices that remarked: "Ele tem voz, até está igual" (He has voice, it is even alike); it paused and continued: "Ele teve um passagem, ele teve vantagem" (He had a passage, he had advantage). Some thirty seconds later, the same masculine voice again intruded into the feminine recitation of words and declared "Sou o Tom!" now at -4, 0 dB. The feminine voice immediately followed with: "Ele tem voz, passar!" (He has voice, pass!).

The voice that vigorously affirms "Sou o Tom!" and the feminine voice that obviously comments on "Sou o Tom", as above described, have been listened to by several dozen people of different nationalities. There was no discrepancy about the content. The linguistic content of "Sou o Tom" is unmistakable even for those who do not understand Portuguese.

Naturally, I was puzzled by this voice and thought who this Tom might be, since I don't know anybody among my friends or acquaintances, anywhere in the world, called Tom. Then it occurred to me that it could be Tom Harrison,

Ann's husband. The more I thought about it, the more sense it made to me. In fact, the content of the feminine voice's talk could entirely apply to him. The voice said "He had a passage, he had advantage". Knowing that the economy of language together with the symbolic use of words seem to be one of the main characteristics of ITC voices in general, I thought [a good passage] was implicit in "he had a passage". And this made perfect sense! Certainly Tom had a good passage because, as the voice said, "he had advantage". And his advantage could very well consist in the teachings and experiences he inherited from, and lived with, his mother and aunt.

If it really was Tom Harrison, the only puzzle remaining was why he spoke in Portuguese, a language he had no knowledge of. I know and speak English perfectly well, so I suppose it was not because he was addressing me. Was it because he was, at the moment he spoke through DRV, working with the Portuguese Group at Rio do Tempo Station? It could be but of course, we cannot be sure. One of my very first DRV voices, a clear feminine voice that closely followed my experimentation for a long time, identified herself as Joan Colbert. She used to speak and reply to me mostly in Portuguese but, sometimes, in English, also. I mean she would say a few words in Portuguese and continue with a sentence in English, for instance. All perfectly clear.

I suppose the most important lesson to learn from the remarkable voice that vigorously stated "Sou o Tom!" is that we really do not understand much of what is going on in the subtle levels of reality. My beloved Doberman dog Nisha was born in India and we used to speak in English to her. However, the little human voice that through DRV identified herself as Nisha, and said a few words, spoke in Portuguese, not in English. When I, in English, requested a confirmation from the little voice asking: "Is it you mummy?" she again replied in Portuguese: "Sim!" (See: the CD for Electronic Voices). Also, on one of the occasions

Professor David Fontana spoke with Rio do Tempo in English, the first reaction of the voices came in Portuguese, "Nós falamos português" (We speak Portuguese) they said. Then proceeded to speak in English.

If we fully assume one of ITC lessons, that is the fact that the intellect does not seem to play any appreciable role in the communication process, while emotions certainly do play a major role, and if we recognise that we know so very little about the things essential, not only of the next world but also of this world, Tom's beautiful affirmation of existence and identity would have served a great purpose.

Note: 20/9/2011. I have now listened to the CD (Christmas Party Sitting, 1954) that Ann sent me and listened to Tom's natural voice. On direct listening, both voices are not at all dissimilar. The anomalous voice is much faster as commonly happens and more vigorous, but the timbre seems compatible, considering the recording quality of the 1950s. This is just an informal assessment without any technical implications because real voice comparison must be done by an accredited forensic expert.

Ann's reply: When Anabela sent me the audio clip of 'Sou o Tom' I sent out the thought to him, "What have you been up to now? Did you really do DRV?" The following week, we were sitting in the home circle here in Spain. Barbara, one of the sitters, who knew Tom very well, and is not the main medium, clairaudiently heard Tom say "I can do more than boil an egg now!"

She asked if that meant anything to me – my answer from him, as cryptic as ever. If I left him for a day, the only thing he would make for his lunch was two soft-boiled eggs with fingers of bread, colloquially known as 'soldiers'.

Five days before I had the message through Barbara, on June 16th, when I asked Tom about it at Stewart's circle, this is what he said through Stewart's trance:

Ann: Yes. Have you been experimenting? (*In my mind was the recording and I know how easily our thoughts are picked up in a séance.*)

Tom: Hahahaha (*very breathily*)

June: He's laughing.

Ann: Yes.

Tom: You know the answer to that, Ann.

Ann: I'm looking forward to getting the recording.

Tom: Only give me time, give me time. It is so strange even for me, so strange.

He had found yet another way of communicating. And this time was it with the help of David, his 'blood brother' who knew much more about it?

In Anabela's description of the communication, the use of the word 'passagem' is interesting. Did the voice mean he had a good passing to the spirit world or that he had managed to get through with his message? As Anabela stated in her account of the research that she and others had carried out in Vigo in 2008 a voice, "....said 'Ha passagem' – 'There is passage' – was this a reference to the fact that the voices could get through – It could be interpreted as such."

When translating passagem into the English 'passage' we need to consider the different ways we use the word 'passage'. It could, in the brevity of word usage in their transmission, mean that he had managed to 'Breakthrough' – to connect – to get his voice through because of his knowledge and determination.

Whatever its meaning in this case – he could 'do more than boil an egg now'.

*Twelve*

# Long distance
# cross-correspondence links

Throughout my first summer without his physical presence Tom continued to use our many friends to show how close he is, and distance poses no problem.

In July, an e-mail to a medium friend in the Isle of Wight came back with an evidential message, as Tom tuned-in with her and 'took over' as she was replying to my letter.

> Dear Ann,
>
> So glad you are doing OK and feel Tom around you often. I also believe wholeheartedly he would try to speak to you through Stewart too. There's no question in my mind. I've got no idea who you stood up to, or made your point clear to, in the last 3-4 weeks, but he is chuckling and oh, so proud of you. You know what you want, what makes sense to you and what is for the best – and you have made sure your wishes are known.
>
> He wants you to know he supports everything you are doing and agrees with decisions you have made. He trusts you implicitly and you know that was very important to him. He just thinks you are wonderful and enjoyed every minute of his time with you – and he says – at his age he has a right to be soppy!
>
> Anyway, I just wanted to have a little chat with you but Tom has taken over – not that I mind. We very often think of you and our very enjoyable times spent in the company of you both. ....... Tom says "Cheerio" and so do I.
>
> All very best wishes and kind thoughts.      Julie.

I had to think back to what I had been doing. Then I remembered at the beginning of the month I had driven the 500 miles across Spain to spend time with Frederick and Valerie on the Algarve and so I replied to her:

> Thank you for this lovely message. Three weeks ago when I was with dear friends in Portugal I insisted on staying in the garden and not traipsing all over trying to park by the sea on a busy weekend. They even thanked me for it later – for having time to chat and relax. They are such good hosts, but I did need time to unwind.

Of course, Tom would have been there with us, in a place he loved to visit and with dear friends. On the Sunday morning, we sat together to send out absent healing thoughts and afterwards Frederick relaxed into a trance state and Tom had taken the opportunity to briefly speak to us.

Tom has also continued to work with Gilly.

By the Spring of 2011, she still didn't have the trumpet that Tom had urged her to get and this is what she wrote:

> I went to Cober Hill recently on a Physical Mediumship Course with Dean Kenyon as my tutor. I have sat with him on a number of occasions before. When I sat in the cabinet on the last day, Tom shouted out his name – 'Tom here.' I was in a trance state, but he said that he was interested in the trumpets at the back of the room (two put at the back). Apparently my voice was very different. It was only a short message, but it felt very strong.
>
> I agree with you that he seems to be urging me to get a trumpet I have not got one and I definitely must look for an aluminium one. Lovely to be in touch with you, thank you for everything.
>
> Gilly

I put her in touch with a site on the internet and she bought one. Within a short time I received this email:

> Ann, I have had a couple of short messages from Tom, whilst sitting with Ray. The two of us sit regularly on a Friday morning. I take my newly acquired trumpet — aluminium, of course — and we sit in silence for two hours.
>
> The most recent message went as follows:
>
> 'Sunrise likes this trumpet. It is aluminium, like Tom's. Sunrise is your friend. He joins you with great heat. (YES!) I will bring you strength in communication and honesty and truth. Tom is pleased. Tom is here to help you. He takes an interest in these sittings for spirit. Love to Ann.'
>
> Tom also spoke of a piece of delicate jewellery, like gold filigree (looked like it had pearls on it).
>
> I hope to see you on Stewart's weekend in October.
>
> With Love, Gilly.

I wrote back concerned that they were sitting in silence knowing that physical phenomena appears to thrive on sound, joy and laughter and received this in reply.

> July 27th
>
> Just a few lines before I go on holiday. Ray and I sat last Friday, with music at your and Walter's suggestion, and certainly it raised the vibes and helped communication. The trumpet was with us too. Tom told me that Aunt Agg was connected strongly to the gold filigree and pearl necklace.
>
> When I was looking at his book *Life After Death: Living Proof* the next day I saw on page 149 there is a photograph of Aunt Agg in what looks like the necklace mentioned by Tom. See what you think, Ann. He also talked about a connection with a silver button with military connections, sounded like the Army in India.' .....
>
> It is lovely to correspond with you. You and Tom have been a great help in my development.    Gilly

I agreed with her about the necklace and sent her a better photo of Aunt Agg showing it. I could also confirm that Tom had a connection with a man in the Army in India, Lt. Col Roy Dixon Smith. He had attended their circle in 1948 and met and kissed his wife in materialised form. He recorded all this in his book, *New Light on Survival* published in 1952, but it is also retold in Tom's book. Maybe this was another cryptic clue for me – to tell me he has met up with Roy Dixon Smith?

Gilly wrote also that Tom had shown her a vision of me by a tree, with a cool breeze on my face, and had said 'I will always be at her side.' She said there was something about a wheelbarrow as well, but she didn't remember the details.

I didn't understand the wheelbarrow connection as I don't have one. Shortly before Tom's death we had been given one by friends who were selling up, and returning to England. I found it too heavy to handle by myself and some months before this message I had given it to the man who helped with my garden. Could it be something to do with that?

A couple of days after Gilly had mentioned the wheelbarrow, I had an email from Kate in Blackpool. While she was meditating that afternoon, Tom had made himself known and immediately afterwards she wrote to pass on his message. Amongst many special personal details was this closing image:

"The people sitting on the chairs were singing something about a wheelbarrow going round and round and clapping their hands. I felt love and happiness and sheer joy from them."

Another reference to a wheelbarrow! Was there a connection? Or was it maybe just a link from spirit, using a word that really has no great importance to anything? An incidence of cross-correspondence which had been a popular test of spirit connections, around a hundred years ago.

Maybe our spirit friends were demonstrating that they can pass similar information through different mediums and it need not be a definitive link to me – an intriguing thought.

I suppose the 'wheelbarrow' was going round and round, passing from one owner to another, – whether by spirit links between Gilly and Kate or physically, by me passing on the gifted barrow. However, Gilly later showed me the notes she had made at the time of the sitting, in which she had described seeing me 'pruning the tree' until I had a 'wheelbarrowful'.

I thought back then, to the hot day in late June, when I had cut the long shoots out of the top of the lemon tree to allow the sea breeze to blow in through the Sanctuary window. I love to stand by the window in our Sanctuary, with a lemon tree just a few feet away, enjoying the cooling sea breeze when the summer temperature climbs above 36C. I remembered too, how I had, fleetingly, wished I still had the wheelbarrow to move all the spiny cuttings.

And Tom would definitely have been by my side that day, as he always had been, when I was balanced on top of the tall pair of steps to do the cutting!

So perhaps we have both. A 'cross correspondence' with two mediums, many miles apart, being given slightly different information about the same object – the wheelbarrow, around the same time. Plus my folks in spirit conveying they are aware of what I'm doing –

1. passing on a gift-wheelbarrow.

2. wishing I had one for the prunings from the tree.

Recently, I came across the description in Hannen Swaffer's book *My Greatest Story* of a cross-correspondence test carried out in America, in the 1920s, between 'Margery' Crandon and Sary Litzelman. The two women sat in their different homes, miles apart, and the test was set by some

Naval officers at the Boston Naval dockyard. Maurice Barbanell once wrote that tests of this kind may seem trivial but are the ones demanded by sitters.

That evening, Sary, could not understand, why all she could do was to go to a drawer in which there were half-a-dozen wrist watches. "All I get is watch," she said. At the Crandons' home, where they had been washing a dog, Margery merely said "Dog, dog, dog," then added, "Give me your pen," and wrote down the word 'dog'. "It's a washout," said Button, who was the President of the American Society for Psychical Research. But, the next day, the Navy Yard telephoned to say that their test had been 'dog watch'.

We see in this example the intelligence behind the communication. If it were transmitted by telepathy from the naval officers' minds, the women would both have had the words 'dog watch'. But Sary didn't get a word just had to look at some watches and Margery just said 'dog' which was something with which she had been concerned with that day.

In my instance, Gilly didn't get that I wished I had a wheelbarrow, but that I had pruned until I had a 'wheelbarrowful'. And I had too, and many more lengths besides, all with numerous one-inch thorns!

Kate had seen that the spirit friends were obviously happy as the wheelbarrow went 'round'. Here was another cryptic clue which they love to set me and it wasn't solved until I was writing this section. I realised then what the 'round and round' meant – for I had passed the wheelbarrow on (round) to be used, instead of it standing in a corner, rusting away. A clever link and what appears to be a cross-correspondence!

In that same email of July 27th, Gilly had written that Tom had said – 'A new book is in her head – soon to be on paper.'

This was around the same days as the phrase 'Only Connect' was repeatedly running through my head and Kate had picked up the words from Tom – "Ann book, Ann book," and the following day – "Harrison Connections."

That email of Kate's continued with these words:

> ... Later that day I went on the computer and oh my – the second line of your e-mail was 'there may be a book in it!'. I am totally convinced, Ann that Tom was trying to say that you will write your own book, and I bet this will be on your hubby's material work for spirit and his return from spirit. The 'connections' he has all over the country are giving him the opportunity to prove his 'return' again and again, and with his huge enthusiasm and energy of spirit, he will take every opportunity to keep on doing so. ...

So *this* is the book Tom referred to in Gilly's e-mail which has been slowly building over the months – with him communicating in as many different ways and through as many people as possible, as Micky had told us he would; to be in touch, not only with me, but with others, to support them. These varied connections, with new mediums as well as with those already known to him, increases his expertise in manipulating different energies.

As he had said, the first time he was able to speak through Rob, in the Acacia home circle on May 17th:

> Tom: Hello, dear. I'm managing to get through.
> Ann: Good, Well done!
> Barbara: I would say about time.
> Tom: Still as cheeky as ever!
> B: I wouldn't be any other way.
> T: I wouldn't have you any other way... I'm always around. You know that.
> All: Yes

122

A: Getting to work with different people.

T: Yes it's very interesting, adapting to different energies.

A: Good.

B: We knew you were coming tonight.

T: But I know I'm always welcome here. (Others: Yes.) Don't let them try to tell you otherwise.

A: Rob always knows when you're here.

T: I know and he's the one that's likely to say – 'What the hell are you doing here?' (*laughter from the group*)

A: He said it was about time you came.

Sitter: We miss your hugs. ...your hugs on a Sunday.

T: I'm so happy to be able to speak with you. ... Well, I'm going to try to make it a regular occurrence. ...I have to go. Bless you all.


In early August, Kate wrote again:

> I do keep getting Benidorm. I think this must be his calling card, bless him. And I could see Tom standing on a balcony looking out to sea and smiling and felt his happiness. For me, the best thing was that his words were not an impression – I could hear his voice just as I remembered with that slight accent.
>
> He says tea – and he moved a spoon when you were in the kitchen. Also, you have changed or moved a mat.

Benidorm was our special 'short break' place. Not the crowded bars with their noise, but the beautiful promenade and the good restaurants, where we spent our tenth wedding anniversary. He did so love to be by the sea, and we sat out on the balcony of our hotel room overlooking the sea – sipping the complimentary champagne – with the promenade half-empty and quiet in the May sunshine.

Mmmmm – Happy Days!

But, coming back down to earth, I also remembered, so vividly, how, ten days earlier, the water-softener had clogged and overflowed during the night, pouring gallons of salt water all over the office floor. The carpet was ruined. There was nothing to be done – it had to be removed. This involved emptying the very large, very full stationery cupboard that stood on one edge of it so I could lift the carpet.

Having had a good cry, I set to work. I finished the unwelcome task by washing the floor to get rid of the salt. Then, as I decided to put down two small rugs instead of another carpet, I said to him "It was always so much easier doing things together!"

Looking through my diary of 'happenings' later, I found a note I had made. How, late one afternoon, I had made a cup of tea in a china mug and added the milk. I placed the spoon on the granite worktop – not in the cup – walked away and heard the sound of the spoon 'ping' against the china as though it was being stirred. When I looked the spoon was on the work surface by the mug, but the tea was moving.

A happy memory and a reminder of a recent 'disaster' – 'Trivia' again – but precious support for me.

For fifteen years we had not spent more than one week apart and he wanted to be around me too, for he was having to adjust, the same as I was.

A few days later Kate sent this:

> I sense he is having a bit of fun and wants you to do the same. – He has done something – learnt to fly and has got his pilot's wings. I could see the RAF circles and hear the name John or Johnny. Gosh, there will be no stopping him now. He will be zooming around like one of the Red Arrows.

Four days later, on 11th August, I had a phone call from Violet in Melbourne, Australia, telling me of a sitting she had had the previous evening. For several days, she had been sensing someone around the house – shadows – not quite seeing who it was. She decided to have a table sitting with the closest members of her circle. Very quickly, the table responded to spell out T-O-M – 'My brother?' she asked. NO – H-A-R-R-I-S-O-N. The table shot all over the room and up to the ceiling. When Violet asked if she should tell me about it, the table moved to confirm YES. After much more detailed information for Violet and the other sitters the communicator left.

Later Violet told me he had mentally said to her 'Tell Ann I've connected!' She did not know that 'connect' was the special word he had given me for the book. Again more confirmation.

On August 13th, I had this email from Kate:

> While sitting last night, time and again I kept hearing, 'Table tilting, doing Table tilting. Lifting table.' I could kick myself that I did not voice this because I kept dismissing it as we do not do table tilting. – I was wondering should I say something to the group about having a go, but thought better of it, as time is being taken up with the others practising for trance. Reading your e-mail this morning, surely, Ann, this must have been Tom confirming to you and the Australian link that 'yes' he was the 'pilot' flying the table. – How marvellous and going from one end of the earth to the other to get his confirmation through (no distance for him of course) – it's amazing – What a guy!

It is not quite the old complicated classical cross-correspondences of Frederic Myers and the others, between mediums, of years ago. But these instances show the links he and the spirit team are creating, with the ability to pass intelligent linked information through mediums who have never met nor know of each other.

Another accomplishment. I feel these intelligent links are as good as any done a century ago.

Tom had said to me at Stewart's circle in Hull, in mid-July: "Tell them they haven't seen anything yet!"

The reference in Kate's email to pilot's wings and 'Johnny' links to one of my favourite poems. A wartime poem which was once given to me clairaudiently as a link for someone to a pilot she had known by the name of John!

> For Johnny
>
> Do not despair
> For Johnny-head-in-air;
> He sleeps as sound
> As Johnny underground.
>
> Fetch out no shroud
> For Johnny-in-the-cloud;
> And keep your tears
> For him in after years.
>
> Better by far
> For Johnny-the-bright-star,
> To keep your head,
> And see his children fed.
>
> *John Pudney*

*Thirteen*

# Advance Knowledge

The next connection I learned of was to someone Tom had never met in our physical dimension. Although we had met the physical medium David Thompson on a couple of occasions, seven years earlier, we had never met his companion, Christine Morgan.

In late August 2011, David and Christine (from Sydney, Australia) came to the Acacia Centre in Spain for a week of demonstrations and workshops.

On the Sunday evening after the opening session, I introduced myself. As soon as Christine knew who I was, she excitedly told me of a vision she had had some months earlier, and before she knew I was to be giving Tom's talk on Minnie's Circle at the Festival of Physical Mediumship.

But I'll let her tell you in her own words:

> Early in 2011, whilst lying down, I had a spontaneous clairvoyant image of a man bending down looking at me. I saw him very vividly and heard the words, "I will see you in a séance."
>
> I thought this was very odd, as no-one knows who will communicate in a séance and I had no idea of who the man was. As I sent out the thought as to who it was, a strong impression of the image of the cover of Tom Harrison's book *Life after death* came to me, and I heard the man say, "I am Tom."
>
> I thought this unusual as I had never met him and had never even read the book! I forgot about this until several

months later I found that Ann Harrison, Tom's wife, was going to be at the same event in Spain where I was booked to work!

It then occurred to me that maybe the spirit knew we would be meeting up? I chatted to Ann at the event and described my experience, without telling her the final part about the séance. I had not discussed this with anyone as I was wondering why Tom Harrison would come to me?

However, we were to find out later that week. Tom came through at the first séance and spoke directly to Ann, giving her evidence. Ann stated it was definitely Tom.

I will not forget that experience, and know that without a doubt that Tom was letting me know from the spirit side of life that he would be around that week.

Nobody knew anything about this experience – not even the medium conducting the séance until I told them afterwards.

It was a lovely experience for Ann and myself to once again be reminded of the intelligence of the spirit world.

On that Monday evening, during the first dark séance, Tom materialised and spoke to me in a 'public' séance with thirty-four other people present.

Let me set the scene:

In the wooden building, specially constructed for dark physical séances, there were ten or eleven chairs down each of three sides of the room. On the fourth side, a few feet away from the cabinet, two or three chairs were placed at each side. The cabinet was a tall, three-sided wooden box with curtains hanging from the fourth side which faced into the centre of the circle. Once we were all in place two people, previously unknown to David or his circle members, carried out checks on David and the circle members to make sure they were not hiding anything about their person. All of us going into the séance were subject to the same rigorous checks. The cardigan that David always wears was secured with cable ties through the button holes and its ties checked.

David was fastened into the chair in the cabinet and each fastening over-bound with a cable tie. Christine then gagged his mouth tightly and a cable tie was closed over the knot at the back of his neck. These were all checked and finally, the curtains were dropped over the front of the cabinet.

When this was completed, the checkers took their places, one either side of the cabinet. The male checker sat next to Christine at the left of the cabinet (as we looked at it) and the woman checker sat next to Sarah, on the right. Sarah was a former circle member who was controlling the music player. Their other circle friend sat amongst the rest of the sitters.

After an opening prayer, Christine called for the music and we sang, hummed, lah-lahed – whatever – with gusto to *Search for the hero inside yourself*. We 'doh-did-do'd' to the Irish jig and joined in the bits we knew in *True colours* and *Somewhere over the rainbow*. A great feeling of joy and laughter filled the room. At last, after months of waiting, we were there and we were ready.

We heard a cultured voice speaking and Christine called for us to join hands, which we did. It was William welcoming us all and after speaking for a while he called for questions. When someone asked a question, he would ask if he could approach them and we could hear his solid footsteps as he walked over to them. As he stood in front of them he would ask if he could touch them and a large hand was placed on their head – once or twice the person thought it was two hands it was so large. Occasionally a cheek was stroked too. (David's hands are quite small and he was wearing soft-soled trainers. Everyone else had removed their shoes outside the room, but these moving footsteps were from hard-soled shoes.)

When he returned to the cabinet we were permitted to release hands, which was a relief as they were getting very sweaty on a hot Spanish August evening. In what seemed to be no time, Timmy, the young boy communicator, called for the trumpet. Christine placed it in front of the cabinet. Once we had joined hands again, we were treated to an amazing light display from the luminous band on the large end, as the trumpet was manipulated rapidly from one side of the room to the other; looping and swirling, faster and further than I have witnessed before. It came close to knees and heads, sometimes pausing to prod someone in the chest before it was away again – great fun, causing lots of laughter and again raising the vibrations to a new high. When that was put away into a cover so no light was showing, Timmy went around the circle touching people, prising apart fingers, trying to separate peoples' hands so that they might feel his tiny fingers. Robert described them as being as small as his five-year-old granddaughter's fingers and there was certainly no one as small as that in the room that night.

It was now time for personal contacts and to my delight Timmy asked if there was an 'Ann'.

But let me give it in full:

> Timmy: Is there a lady here called Ann?
> Ann: Yes there is.
> Timmy: Eh missis, I haven't spoken to you before?
> Ann: No, you haven't.
> Timmy: There's a gentleman who I spoke to before I came through who knew you and he said he knew other people here too.
> A: Yes, there are.
> Timmy: He said 'Can I come through and speak to my wife and friends?'

A: It would be lovely. (*and everyone else said* 'Ahhhh!')

Timmy: An' I said I'll see what I can do and I'll tell you something, (A: Yes.) missis. He had this big Indian with him, (A: Yes.) an' I was a bit frightened!

A: There's no need to be frightened he's a lovely man. He looks after everyone. He's a good friend.

Timmy: He said can he bring him as well, and I was too frightened to say no.

A: That really is one of the best …

Timmy: I'll see if we can get him through.

A: That would be brilliant.

Christine (CM): Just keep hold of hands, please.


There were then the sounds of ectoplasm being extracted like a heavy vomiting sound. As people started to chatter Christine asked us to wait a moment. A voice then said 'Darling' in a most strangulated way.

A: Come on, Darling.

Barbara and Debbie who both knew Tom called out: 'Come on Tom.'

A: Come on, Sweetheart.

Tom: Hello, Love. (*weakly*)

Debbie and others cheer.

A: I can feel you getting very close.

Tom: Is that you, Ann?

A: It is. Come along, Sweetheart.

Tom: You know, I should know.

A: I know.

Tom: I've got someone with me.

A: I know you have Sunrise with you. (*overlapping*)

Tom: I've got Sunrise with me. He's going to come through.

A: That's lovely.

I cannot make out Tom's words in the following few exchanges on the recording and in my emotion I cannot remember them, but we continued our chat:

> A: Did you enjoy this afternoon? (*a reference to me doing a talk about his mother's mediumship*)
>
> Tom: Aye I did …. The woof! (*Sunrise's sound as he prepared to speak*)
>
> A: I was just as bad as you at timing!
>
> Tom: … the recordings.
>
> A: No, I didn't.
>
> Tom: I was beside you all the time.
>
> A: I knew you were. I knew the way I was telling the stories.

In the complete darkness, two hands were placed, unerringly, either side of my head and he kissed me on the forehead. A smacking kiss that all could hear. (All. Ohhhh!)

> A: He held my head and kissed my forehead.
>
> Rob/ Debbie: Well done, Tom.
>
> Tom: You know I always was sensitive, wasn't I?
>
> A: Yes.
>
> Tom: I didn't let others see it.
>
> A: I know, but you were, very, very sensitive – cried at all the films.
>
> Tom: Don't tell all our secrets. (*laughter, particularly loud from Robin to which Tom responded*) Robin, lad!
>
> A: Yes, Robin's there.
>
> Robin: Hello, Tom!
>
> Tom: Robin, lad.
>
> Robin: Nice to hear you.
>
> (*At this, Tom moved away from me and walked across to the other side of the room, good 5-6 metres away.*)
>
> Tom: Robin, how are you?
>
> Robin: Fine, thank you, Tom. How are you?

Tom: This ectoplasm's difficult.

Robin: Yes, you got to practise a lot, I would imagine.

Tom: I never thought it would be so hard to come through.

Robin: Oh right. (*Tom says something which is unintelligible*) Yes, that's very good. Thank you for coming. (*Tom continues to speak, but I can't make it out on the recording*) Yes, absolutely.

Tom: Is that Rob?

Rob: Hello, Tom. How are you doing in the spirit world? Are you busy?

Tom: I surely am. Not as ……. here.

Rob: You never change, Tom.

Tom: Ann.

A: Yes, Darling?

Tom: I love you. (*from all* 'Ohhhh!')

A: I love you too very, very much.

Tom: I'll speak to you again.

A: Yes. Very soon.

Tom: Oh! not too soon. (*The 'Oh' sounding very much like Granny Lumsden's Northern accent on the recording of the Christmas Party in 1954!!*)

A: Not on your side you'll …. (*drowned out by laughter*)

Tom: So good to see you, so glad I could come through.

A: OK, I know.

Rob: Goodbye, Tom.

Robin and others: Bye Tom!

Then the same gurgling sound of the ectoplasm going as coming and we heard heavy footsteps on the tiled floor.

Ann: Come on, friend. (*heavy footsteps approached as though with hard soles.*) Come on, my friend.

Sunrise: My Little Sister.

A: My dear friend, it's so good to hear you.

S: It is Sunrise.

A: Yes, I can hear it is. I can feel the cold air here. (*The column of cold felt so tall in front of me.*)

S: Blessings!

A: Thank you, my blessings to you. I remember you well.

S: You do my work much justice.

A: Thank you. You worked very well with that circle. I know you still do. It is good to hear you.

*He then begins to chant very loudly in a North American Indian language which I believe he then translated as, –* "The Spirit is amongst you and around you."

Robin: Thank you, Sunrise.

Many others echoed this and we heard the sounds – the sucking back – of dematerialisation. Not a sound an unamplified human voice box could have made, if at all.

Our first direct contact.

I believe Tom found it difficult because of the emotion of being together again. He always felt things deeply and as he said to me 'I always was sensitive.' He did easily become emotional, especially in the film *Ghost*.

As he released me and walked across the room to speak to Robin and Robert, his voice became stronger and more like his normal voice. This was so pronounced that one lady from Switzerland, who has watched his video *Visitors from the Other Side* more than five times, said it was definitely recognisable as Tom Harrison's voice. This was backed up by Barbara, whom with Robert we have known since 2002, so they know Tom well – and it was so very different from David's London/Australian twang.

It was just too wonderful! Even after years of sitting with Stewart Alexander, and having the materialised Dr Barnett play with my hair, and Walter lift my hand and kiss it –

nothing can compare with having this special privilege of having my love and our special friend there in front of me.

I was not the only one that night to have a personal contact. Another lady there had a meeting with her father, whom she hardly knew on the earth, but he reminded her of an incident with a pet rabbit when she was very young – another very emotional true reunion.

\* \* \* \* \*

On the Thursday evening, Christine and David gave a demonstration of mental mediumship. Towards the end of the evening, after a number of messages to others present, Christine announced that she had to give in to Tom, who had been pestering her to communicate with me. She had a wonderful amount of evidence for me – 'trivia' you might again say, but fun and very meaningful:

– from the state of his spectacles – 'mucky' she said. (*Just as I used to before I gave them a good soapy wash*);

– to a stubbly, rough chin, and she stroked hers just as he did (*to check if he needed a shave before a bedtime cuddle*);

– a bottle of rum? – (*for a 'shot' in our winter morning hot chocolate*);

– a colourful tie I had kept – (*his wedding tie – for our wedding and then worn at Chris and Hannah's eleven years later*);

– you still have a special sweater (*the first I had bought him, his favourite, indestructible 'snowflake' design*);

– and a blazer (*Bowls National Umpire's red blazer which is still in the wardrobe*).

This further contact by Tom I feel was also a validation of their physical mediumship. If there had been anything suspect with the physical mediumship earlier, there would have been no question of him wanting to work with her mentally on the Thursday and coming through with such special unknown details.

A truly special event at the Acacia Centre.

*The séance room at the Acacia Centre is the large wooden building on the left of the picture. The Centre itself, for demonstrations of mediumship, services and workshops is the building in the centre of the picture beyond the trees.*

*Fourteen*

# "He will hold your hand"

You might think it was difficult to top that, but three weeks later, in mid-September, I found myself back at the home circle in Hull. I had to take my friends to the airport in Alicante and as there were seats available on the flight, I decided to join them. They lent me their second car – a beautiful Rover75 automatic and having stayed the night with them I drove over to Hull for the sitting.

At the start of the evening Tom spoke through Stewart, still concerned whether we could hear him:

> Tom: Can you hear?
>
> Ann: Yes clearly.      Katie: Yes.
>
> Ann: Even Katie can hear you. (*Katie is severely deaf but spirit have devised a method in the séance room by which she can hear.*)
>
> T: Well good old Katie!
>
> K: Hello Tom, lovely to hear you again.
>
> T: I ... this is like old times. I know that ... Ohh ...  I know what I want to say, but it's so hard – it's so very difficult to say a single word.
>
> A: Well you are saying plenty of them. You are doing very well, Love.
>
> T: Oh am I?
>
> June: Yes.
>
> Carol: Very clear, Tom.
>
> T: Ann, darling, I'm so happy that you are here.

A: Yes, so am I, so am I.

T: You know, people will not understand the difficult ... the difficulty in saying what ... making myself understood ... so hard but I want you to know ... I want you all to know that all is fine here ... all is fine. I've met so many people ... Wonderful. I'm often with Gaynor, very often. I know that Cober is not far off.

A: That's right.

T: Be sure to give everyone my love.

A wonderful night back among special friends, and especially so as later that evening Tom materialised. This time it was alongside Dr Barnett, who regularly materialises to give healing. For several years, he gave healing to Tom, whenever we sat in Hull, and also to Jackie, our friend, as I have already mentioned.

Katie Halliwell and I were sitting next to each other in the circle. We heard a materialised form moving out of the cabinet into the room, and Katie announced that two hands were tapping on her head. At the same time the fingers of two hands were tapping, as though playing the piano, on my head. When I told everyone that I also had someone in front of me, Dr Barnett, to my right, said "Ann, my dear, there is no purpose in me spelling out to you whose hands they are."

For the 'experiment' that evening they had two people out of the cabinet, some 5-6 feet distance from the medium. This was most unusual, and the second person was Tom. He played with my hair before moving his hand down my arm and tapping my knee. Then he picked up my left hand and cradling it between his two slim hands with their long fingers, I heard his familiar, emotional, "Oh, oh, oh," as he tried to speak to me. But he could not control the energy needed to hold the form together and the ectoplasm returned to the medium in the cabinet.

Instantly, I found larger hands were holding my outstretched hand. Hands I felt I recognised, Walter's hands. As he took control, he spoke just one familiar word "Well."

The fact that Walter was also out in the room amazed us.

> June: Is that you, Walter?
>
> Walter: It is folks.
>
> J: Hello, Walter.
>
> W: Ann, I want you to know this ma'am. That it would have been expecting rather too much for Tom to speak in addition to forming into materialisation, OK.
>
> A: He did very well.
>
> W: Folks, but I tell you this, that I would much rather speak through Stewart. It is darned difficult.
>
> Dr B: I would like to begin again.
>
> W: OK. OK. Folks, I find this to be quite extraordinary.

Had we had *three* materialised forms or part forms there?!

So the experiment began again. Tom was not deterred; moments later the form built again, and we could hear the effort it was for him to walk out of the cabinet.

He had always told us that spirit had said carrying ectoplasm on their etheric bodies was like climbing out of a swimming pool in a sodden overcoat.

Knowing it was Tom, June told him not to try to move far, just speak.

> Tom: Ann.
>
> Ann: I know you are here, love. You are doing so well.
>
> Tom: Wonderful. Oh, my love!
>
> A: Yes, my darling.
>
> T: If I say nothing else ... I... I want you to know this... that I am so settled, so settled. Miss you, miss you.
>
> A: I miss you too.
>
> Carol: We do miss you, Tom.

T: It's wonderful, wonderful. Ann, you know I'm often with you.

A: I know you are.

T: Oh, Oh! (*emotionally*)

A: I think you did something special? (*I held a strong thought in my mind of my crystal swan.*)

T: Yes, yes!

A: That was a lovely surprise.

And with a characteristic thump on the floor, as the ectoplasmic form collapsed, – he was gone.

That was almost the end of the sitting for that evening. Moments later, Walter returned to speak through Stewart's trance – which he had told us he preferred:

W: Folks we did our best. You know that for us, the process can be most frustrating. Those in ignorance of such matters may feel that the process should be simple. It is not, far from that. The fact that Tom was able to come to you, Ann – that in itself, is a virtual miracle.

A: Yes, I understand.

W: And I think that it demonstrates quite clearly the love that he has for you. (A: And me for him.) He made great efforts. Okay folks.

Six months after Kate had told me there would be a special occasion – that he would have his best bib and tucker on, and I would feel him hold my hand – it had happened, just three days short of the eighteenth anniversary of our meeting. A very special anniversary present!

And what had been the something special I asked him about? On September 7th, as I was finishing the final chapter for the book, *Of Love between Two Worlds*, I went from the office into the Sanctuary, which is also our library. I needed the Hannen Swaffer booklet *My Talks with the Dead*, to check the passage about Lady Segrave receiving strength to get through her grief by regular communication with her husband. On opening the door, I found to my amazement – no horror! – my tiny crystal swan, a much-loved sixtieth-birthday present from South Africa, almost on the edge of the shelf, five-six inches from where it normally stood. It could so easily have been knocked off!

Not only that, but the glass-block with a design of dolphins in it had been moved back by two inches against another glass block.

*The white outlines indicate the original positions of the small swan and the block where there was no surface dust.*

How can I be so specific? – Because of the clear marks in the dust where they normally stood. I am not the world's best at dusting, particularly when I become involved in a book. The surface had not been dusted for some weeks, and the windows had been open, allowing the constant fine dust to filter in through the mosquito netting and coat all surfaces.

There was no trail of a drag mark through the dust so these items had been picked up and moved, not dragged and they were absolutely in my eye-line as I entered the room. If they had been like that before I would have seen them. It was as though someone had said "I'm here."

Nor were there any other marks in the dust, which there would have been if I had put something down, and had moved the swan or the block aside. And yes – there was *undisturbed* dust under the swan and the block!

Knowing how he picks up my thoughts I'm sure that 'Yes, Yes' was my answer. If it wasn't Tom who moved them, I'm sure it was done on his behalf, as an added support, showing just how close they are at any time.

*Fifteen*

# Only a thought away

Many times we are told those we love are – 'only a thought away'. In the piece by Canon Scott Holland, he writes – 'Speak to me in the easy way which you always used…'

So I did and do.

I chat to Tom as though he is still here in the physical dimension. One day in the May of my first solo summer, I asked him a question.

I wrote earlier that Anabela lives in the northwest corner of Spain, by the Atlantic Ocean, with a very different climate from me on the south-east coast, bordering the Mediterranean. It is usually raining with her when it is warm and sunny in my part of Spain. So during a phone call one day she asked, as usual, what the weather was like in my area. As it was early May, it was in the mid-twenties celsius with clear blue skies. I told her it was beautiful, my idea of heaven – 'warm enough to sit in the shade all day'.

Amused at my answer, she went on to tell me that she had asked her communicators at Rio do tempo, in a session with the radios, what David Fontana's first impression of the world of spirit had been. The answer had come swiftly back – "The temperature."

Immediately after our conversation I said to Tom – "What do you think to the temperature?"

I didn't have long to wait. The following Tuesday (May 17th), in the home circle with Rob and Barbara I became aware of Tom being very close, as did Barbara. Rob meanwhile, in deep trance, was unaware of our conversation. Barbara heard Tom say to her that at least he didn't have to wear long trousers anymore! When she told me, I laughed and explained the reason for his comment and how during the week I had asked him what he thought of the temperature there. Now I had my answer. He had received my question and he was telling me it was warm in the spirit world – my 'heaven'.

Thirty minutes later, as he spoke through Rob, who had been in deep trance throughout, I asked him if he was finding the temperature pleasant there and he replied:

> T: Yes I told you. I'm wearing my shorts ... Excellent!
> B: No more long trousers, eh Tom?
> T: Never again... (*laughter from us*) I have to go.
> All: Thanks/ Love you, etc.

That was wonderful confirmation, as I had not mentioned to any of them what Anabela had said, nor what I had asked him. He did so love being in shorts, without the drag of material across his knees and he would wear them as long as he could throughout the Spanish year. He took some persuading that long trousers would be needed in England whenever we went back to see the family.

My second try at this telepathy was in June, after Anabela had told me of the recording she had made. I sent out the question "What have you been up to now? Did you really do DRV?" Back again came an answer in the home circle through Barbara "I can do more than boil an egg now!" (as I have already recounted in Chapter 11).

Now I knew how an answer would come back. Not directly to me, as my logic would say it was my imagination – wishful thinking – what I want to hear, and it would have been no proof of his survival. It has to come back through a third party who does not know I have even asked the question.

Tom's own particular way of giving me proof of survival – is to answer these freshly posed questions with statements that only he would give. It may also be in a cryptic form – just like the crosswords we did together.

For me, this proves that the personality has survived physical death and does indeed live on.

Mind-to-mind communication is a two-way connection, for as well as going out, in the form of requests, prayers and questions, there can be information coming in.

Many people call them 'intuitions' – those odd out-of-the-blue thoughts – like the 'Only Connect, Only Connect'. But where do they come from? Are they figments of our imagination – and just what is that imagination?

Or are they communications from the spirit world?

Probably both. For we do know that the mind can access information of its own volition, but we may not be aware when a spirit person is actually passing a thought, an idea, through to us. When a medium is passing on a message is he/she picking up the information from the recipient's mind (psychically) or from the deceased (a spirit contact)? It depends on the content.

Let me digress from Tom's story for a moment.

When I first started on my voyage of discovery over twenty years ago I had heard that mediums could 'read your mind' and convince you that what they told you came from someone you were grieving for. The first detailed message I received, and several others after that, contained information that I had no knowledge of, and I which had to ask others to verify.

In 1990, my first husband, Norman, passed with an uncontrollable cancer, and three weeks later he returned, through a medium in a spiritualist church at Morley, West Yorkshire, some sixty miles distance from me. The medium passed a message from him to a friend of his sister, to say "Tell Bess, you can't believe how good it is – the pain has gone." This friend did not know that Norman had died, nor that Bessie's name, within the family, was shortened to Bess, but she did acknowledge that she had a friend Bessie whose brother was ill. She contacted Bess and the message was relayed to me.

I was impatient to go there, but it was some weeks before Bess and her friend were able to take me to the Morley church, where no one knew me. There I received a message about my father who by then had had a stroke, but I was told that he would walk again – which he did.

On return home, I asked Hull tourist information office for the address of a spiritualist church in Hull. Within three weeks of attending that little church, as they announced that the mediums for the following weekend were Bill and Pat Campbell, I heard inside my head "Pat'll have it. Pat'll have it!" – and she did. The Campbells, a husband and wife team, were mediums from Sheffield, completely unknown to me, and they were very good.

I was given the most wonderful personal evidence that Norman was there, and she concluded the message by giving me information of which I knew nothing, and she said as much – I had to ask. The details given about my husband's uncle were exact – and, as my sister-in law verified, were from their childhood, years before I was born, details he had never told me.

So, this meant the medium was not reading my mind. The information had to come from somewhere else and as she had no knowledge of me or the family, where had it come from? I firmly believe it had come from the dimension where life continues. But was the voice I had heard in inside my head telepathy or what?

Forward now twenty years to 2010.

Late one afternoon, just four weeks after Tom had passed, I was sitting in his chair in the office working on figures, to start the long process of transferring Tom's half of the house into my name. I had put the potatoes on to boil, set the timer (which doesn't always ring!) and become engrossed in the paperwork. Time passed and I became aware of a sharp pain in the back of my head – the same place as he had hit his head – so I asked him what he wanted to tell me – nothing came into my head. Then suddenly, as though it was shouted – I sensed a strong thought – "Potatoes!" I left the office and went through to the kitchen to rescue the potatoes just before they boiled dry, and I stayed to finish preparing the meal, but I could hear odd sounds from his chair in the office so I joked with him about adding the figures up for me.

Three days later, at the Sunday service Morag spoke of a special chair that Tom had and how he often sat in it – another confirmation for me of his presence. The office chair was very old and had come with him when he moved to be with me in Yorkshire. He had spent many hours in it, writing his book and emailing friends. A very special chair, which I now use and most of this book has been written there.

The phrase 'Only Connect' was persistently repeated in my head throughout one afternoon. But it took two emails from a more 'connected' Kate to work out what it was all about – plus a back-up from Violet in Australia that he had 'connected'. This was confirmation indeed that it was a telepathic message from Tom in spirit.

We used to try out telepathy here, occasionally. Not very successfully it must be said, when trying to get the other one to bring back fish and chips for lunch, or add something to the shopping list. The best result we had was at the Arthur Findlay College, during an 'Experimental Week' some years ago. The Scottish psychical researcher, Tricia Robertson, was trying out one of the tests they had used on 'selected mediums' in a Research Project. One partner of a pair of people went into another part of the College at Stansted whilst the other remained in the main lecture room and quietly tuned-in to what their partner was sending. I could see a small ornate clock on a mantelpiece – success, Tom was in the small 'tutors' lounge' and was looking at the little clock in there – on the mantelpiece!


Now Tom is in the spirit world, where we are told, all is thought and on a different vibration, he is certainly having a go at making it work.

Occasionally a 'thought' comes in which I ignore because I don't always hear it as a word inside my head I think that it is just my own thought.

When Kate, Greta and Marie came for a holiday in Spain in March 2011, I took them to the service at the Acacia Centre. On the second Sunday of their holiday, during the service, I had the thought 'take them to the Mar Menor'. It had not been good weather throughout the week they were in Spain and that day the sun was shining. A walk along the promenade would be particularly nice with the sun shining off the water of this almost land-locked lagoon. But I could not remember how to get to it from the road we would be on from the Centre.

I dismissed the idea and we drove back northwards, on the motorway, towards San Miguel, for lunch at the very good Spanish restaurant we had been to the week before.

As we came off the slip road and went over the flyover to turn for San Miguel, I found myself thinking deeply about something that had just been said in the car. I was not conscious of driving for the next three kilometres until I saw the sign for the tunnel! We were back on the motorway heading south again – and now I knew how to get to the Mar Menor!

Had it been telepathy – distraction 'overshadowing' which caused my slip of concentration? The topic broached had nothing to do with the previous conversation so I don't know, but we had a lovely stroll on the promenade in the sunshine before driving to the chosen restaurant for lunch. I cannot say that it was Tom because I have not had backup confirmation of this, but he did love that walk and would not have wanted them to miss it.


The second time I was redirected was three months later, in June 2011, when I returned to England for Jackie's funeral. I flew into Leeds-Bradford airport and hired a car. Having set my 'Sat-Nav' for the M62 to Hull, I set off. The route took me on roads and motorways around Leeds. Suddenly, knowing I should be going straight ahead, thoughts of Eric came into my mind and I found myself turning up the slip road and heading, the sign said, for the City Centre.

Panic! – How on earth did I get back on to my road?

At the next roundabout, I saw a sign for A64 and Wetherby. Now, that I recognised. Ignore the device's instructions, I now knew how to get to where I was going. The traffic was slow and heavy, but as the miles went by I 'realised' that the road I was on went past the turning to Eric's house. I now had the opportunity of seeing him before the funeral the following day.

I spent a special time talking with him, and was able to give him a few minutes healing, for strength for what I knew would be an ordeal the following day. I was then able to drive on to my brother's home thirty miles away.

I am sure Tom had a hand in that because it was exactly what he would have done for such a close friend.

The funeral and reception the next day were crowded with so many people that I am grateful to have had that time with Eric. And I know I can say here "Thank you Tom for influencing me."

I have no proof of Tom's direct intervention for these two incidents, but when chatting to a friend about telepathy recently, she told me that frequently she finds herself buying something in the Supermarket and saying 'I don't know why I'm buying that but Hey-ho!' Then when she gets home her husband – the cook in their house – will say 'Oh good we need that for tonight's meal.' So it seems that, even in our physical world, received thoughts need not get to the conscious stage for those in tune with each other.

One Wednesday in mid July 2013, I was chatting with Robert and Barbara for a little while before we were to start the weekly Healing Service when Barbara found she had Tom close by. He was telling her I had to slow down or I would be having a 'near miss' – or, she asked, had I already had one?

But it wasn't just about the car – "…you have to slow yourself down too, and take your time, relax and enjoy the journey. If you give someone a deadline and they don't make it with the material, tough! It doesn't get published. You have to have your limits and don't work overtime."

A near-miss? Yes, five days earlier, just one hour into the nine-hour drive across Spain to the Algarve, to visit our friends for a long weekend, I had had a near-miss with a truck at a junction. I didn't know traffic would be coming off the motorway on the same slip road as I joined it and I turned right in front of an exiting truck. – (there are a few of these dangerous cross-over junctions in Spain and this junction was new to me.) I am always driving on the limit, wanting to make the journey as short as possible and that's when things can happen.

On the day Barbara spoke to me, on the way to the Centre for the Healing Service, I was on the speed limit again as I was a bit late. I found myself thinking 'I ought to be taking more care of the car and not be pushing it all the time. Parts wear out with over use and hard use; it isn't a racing car and it is now nine years old and I need it to last a long time yet.'

Now, here was Barbara passing on the same words from Tom. Words he would also have said to me when I became frustrated at trying to get a publishing project finished and was working late into the night.

Maybe soon, I will learn to realise that the out-of-the-blue 'ordinary' thoughts may be coming from him to guide me, without him having to make the back of my head tingle to show he is near, and I am very happy for my life to be quietly guided in this way. That doesn't mean I don't and can't have thoughts of my own, but it does mean I still have that contact to check out my ideas.

Over twenty years ago I was given a fascinating book called *Atlas of the Supernatural* which, in the section about Russia (p. 160), states:

In the 1960s the Soviet astrophysicist Dr Nicholai Kozyrev originated a theory of time which he believed would begin to explain the nature of ESP (extra-sensory perception). It involves a previously unknown form of energy which Kozyrev postulates as being denser near to the receiver of (say) a psychically transmitted message and thinner near the sender. He believes that this energy *is* time, and that the power of thought can physically affect it: his equipment has recorded changes which relate more strongly to emotional than calculated thought, for example.

Telepathy, he hypothesizes, depends on the physical density of time, and those people who are particularly good at sending telepathic messages seem to have some way of (unconsciously) making time thin around themselves, and denser round the recipients of the messages. Kozyrev's theory is complex and speculative – but he is not alone in proposing it: the American theoretical physicist Dr Charles A. Muses suggested in 1963, that time, 'although subjective, has quantitatively measurably characteristics' and 'may be defined as the ultimate causal pattern of all energy release.'

So, if we are to understand, as our friends in the spirit world tell us, that they live beyond time, then maybe that explains how, if the essence is 'thin' around them, that messages can be transmitted from them to receptive mediums here. But how our thoughts get through to them – that is a different matter. Unless it is that our emotive, loving thoughts create a thinner time-barrier, as is suggested. Or maybe they 'listening in' anyway as soon as a 'flag' goes up that we are thinking of them.

I had an instance of this in June 2012. I had been persuaded to republish a book by Alan Crossley, who had been Stewart's mentor for some years, helping his physical mediumship to develop. In the book *A Journey of Psychic Discovery* I found a couple of unclear/inaccurate statements that I felt needed to be clarified. I wondered what was I to do and could I do it.

Help was at hand. Towards the end of the hour-long sitting during my visit to see Maureen and Ray Bailey a few days later, I told Ray I wanted to ask a question about a book I was redoing because there were errors in it. Immediately, Ray told me Tom was telling him that I should do it and instantly followed this by saying "Crossley." Very surprised, he said "but that's Alan Crossley and he's here with Tom! He's saying it is very important that the book is right and you MUST change it. He does so want it out in print." Tom had then added – "so do it." Ray had known both Tom and Alan Crossley well, as they were all in the Noah's Ark Society in the early 1990s. I had mentioned nothing to Ray previously about the book nor the problem.

For Alan Crossley to be there with Tom at that – for us – impromptu sitting they must have picked up my deliberations, and though no question had been asked of them – he had been there, ready. And I was guided to make the adjustments by just adding Publisher's Footnotes.

Shortly after writing this chapter, I was asked to do a reading for the Acacia Centre's Sunday service. So, sitting in our Sanctuary I sent out a thought "Well, what do you want me to read?" Instantly I *knew* I had to use something from *Facts*, one of the books dictated to Anthony Borgia from the spirit world. 'Deciding' to look at the chapter on *Prayer*, I quickly found the passage I had to read and it was also Monsignor's words to complete this chapter on thoughts, from the spirit world's point of view:

> In the spirit world, thought has a tangible effect. It is visible to us where it is invisible to you. You can never see the immediate effect of your thoughts. Here in the spirit world, we always do. Although we can speak to one another through the medium of sound, just in the same

way, as do you upon the earth-plane, our best-liked and generally adopted method of personal communication is by the thought process.

One of my earliest experiences in company with my friends, Edwin and Ruth (the former of whom met me upon my transition), was when Edwin spoke to Ruth and me from some distance away. Hitherto we had used our earthly method of speech. But now a light flashed before us, and we heard the sound of Edwin's voice speaking clearly to us. His thought had travelled to us instantaneously, and we fully understood it, just as you understand each other's voices upon the earth-plane.

Edwin's thoughts had passed to us unfailingly and unerringly, and so we had received them. Now this function of thought transference is not confined exclusively to inhabitants of the spirit world nor are we the only people who are able to practise it. Every human being can do so.

It is possible – and perfectly natural – for people still living in the earth world to direct their thoughts to some friend in the spirit world, and they are always doing so. If those thoughts are directed with the full intention that they should be received by the person concerned, then received they will be, beyond any doubt whatever. In the reverse direction, we can send our thoughts to you. They will be bound to reach you, but unless you are sufficiently sensitive psychically you will not be aware of receiving them, or on receiving them, you will not be aware whence they have come. Many people will just consider that some relevant or irrelevant thought has 'come into their head'.

In the spirit world, thought is not necessarily seen as it were, in transit. If that were so the whole of the spirit realms would be criss-crossed with a maze of coloured shafts of light of varying degrees of intensity and colour. While such an effect might be curious, and, indeed, pretty to look upon at first sight, after a time it would become too distracting and confusing to the mind – thought, therefore, is mostly invisible in transit.

But the results of certain concentrations of thought can be felt by us all here in a collective sense. During times of festivity on the earth-plane, such, for example, as at Christmas-tide, when in normal times the earth world breathes forth the greatest measure of goodwill, and when many folks' minds turn towards their friends in the spirit lands, during such festive periods we are keenly aware of a great ascension of kindly thoughts. Such thoughts spread themselves over these realms like a great mantle of affection and joyousness.

That is the result of combined efforts of thought. ...

Thoughts, whether private or collective, must, without failure, be positively directed to the person or persons for whom they are intended. If we do not receive your thoughts, it is because you have not directed them with firm and precise intention.

We, as the percipients, are blameless in the matter.

We might receive but half of your thought, the remainder having no motive power behind it because the mind has wandered along other paths, and thus the full thought has failed to reach us. Those of us who are in active communion with our friends upon the earth-plane enjoy many a good laugh when some friend starts to speak to us clearly and coherently, only for the thought to become weaker and weaker, finally to ramble off into silence. If you could see this happening, I know you would laugh too!

However, in passing, let me say that we can often guess the remainder by filling in the omissions for ourselves.

Or perhaps we might send back an answering thought for you to 'clear the line' to allow your thoughts an unobstructed path.

And how often that does happen even when we are determined to be single-minded in our prayers and healing times?

## The right-hand symbol of 'Goodwill';
## the left-hand symbol of 'Fraternal Love'.

*Notes from my diary: July 20th, 2011*

Was this another gentle telepathic nudge?

This morning I sat in the Sanctuary reading Georgina Brake's story in preparation for the book about her life, *Of Love between Two Worlds* and I found myself thinking about the Spiritualist Lyceum, as she had mentioned 'banners'. Last Friday in Kate's circle, one of the sitters said she could see an 'arch' which made her think about the Lyceums. This set Kate thinking, and she wrote to ask if Tom was connected with the Spiritualist Lyceum. '

He certainly was, but he had never mentioned 'banners'.

Kate had told me weeks before, if I would take time to 'sit and stare' he would come close to me and I believe that is what he did to solve a puzzle that had vexed us for years.

The thought about banners, made me pick up the very old copy of the *Lyceum Manual* that Tom had given me. I couldn't seem to find anything about the banners, but the book then 'opened' at the *'Golden Chain Recitations'* and my eyes fell upon a passage entitled – 148 *The Origins of the Lyceum.* I started to read.

Part way down the second page was a paragraph which struck a chord. In Tom's talk, he always spoke about a special night when Alfred Kitson, the father of the English Lyceum, materialised in their circle. It was the twenty-third anniversary of the opening of Middlesbrough Spiritualist church, which Mr Kitson had conducted, and Charles and Annie Hudson (Tom's in-laws) had been there. They were also present in the home circle that night.

This materialisation by Alfred Kitson was reported in the *Two Worlds* magazine and soon after Tom received a letter, from a close friend of Alfred Kitson. The two men had made a pact, so that if he returned to any circle his identity could be confirmed by a secret saying.

Although, Kitson did not actually manifest in their circle again, they had a message through Sunrise a few months later. He told them that Alfred Kitson was there and sent them this message – 'Right-hand symbol of Goodwill, Left-hand symbol of Fraternal Love.'

It was confirmed by Kitson's friend, George Mack that this was their secret sign.

Tom and I had puzzled over this handshake business often, and although Tom was a strong Lyceumist he could not place this saying, though he often quoted it in his talks.

Today I believe he had at last found the answer and pointed me in the right direction. In a section written by Alfred Kitson himself it says:

> He [Andrew Jackson Davis] saw the Lyceum members marching in perfect order, over undulating plains, with banners waving, and making the valleys resound with their sweet melodies, while on their way to visit some other Lyceum, who received them with friendly greetings giving either the right hand symbol of 'Goodwill'; or the left hand symbol of 'Fraternal Love'.

This was the vision described by Andrew Jackson Davis at the Broadway Hall, New York, in January 1863.

Has Tom talked with 'Dad' Kitson or George Mack in the spirit world? I may have to wait a long time to find out but at least I have my answer to the puzzle.

In our quiet times, they tell us they will draw close and can pass on their information. In this way, another puzzle has been solved.

*Sixteen*

# One year on!

In the first year of our physical separation, Tom had communicated through more than twenty-five different mediums, – through mediums during our Sunday services; in private sittings with friends who are mediums and those just developing. He had also spoken through three good trance mediums and materialised twice, to pass messages to me.

As I gave my talk at the October seminar at Cober Hill in 2011, telling them of his returns within the year, four people attending the seminar came to tell me of their experiences of Tom returning to them personally.

*Ann with a chart showing Tom's 'connections' in the first year, during her talk at the seminar, October 2011.*

Peter from Devon recounted how Tom had sent him a message of encouragement when he was particularly low. Rose and Christine had a message from him at Gateshead church, telling them he would be with them at 'Cober' (the seminar). And June in Cromer told me of a message from him telling her to 'keep going' when she was trying to make a decision about her work.

During the workshop time that Saturday afternoon, I attended the mediumship class and Tom took the opportunity to work through four different people, giving them what may be considered as inconsequential snippets, but most pertinent to me, and unknown to them. In one experiment the medium was blindfolded and the recipient had to stand behind them. The medium who knew Tom slightly, sensed his energy, and he immediately said "I know who I have here so I must have his wife standing behind me." That is how distinctive Tom's energy still is.

However, the highlight of the weekend was during the meal before the Saturday evening séance. Carol, one of Stewart's home circle sitters, who had joined us especially for the sitting that evening, raised her glass in a toast and said "Happy Days!"

I was stunned. I asked her why she had used those words. She had no idea – she had never ever said them before.

Those words were the only toast that Tom and I ever made between us and she had no idea of it. He was clearly showing us he was there with us, even if it wasn't possible to get through in the séance.

A wonderful moment and it really put the seal on the year.

*Seventeen*

# Telekinesis or things on the move!

One of our favourite films is *Ghost*, and in particular the scenes where Patrick Swayze's character is shown how he must concentrate his thoughts to move a physical object. I think that must be pretty much what it is like.

Experiments have been carried out in laboratories to influence random numbers on a computer screen, with some success. For many years, there have been instances where physical objects have been observed to be moved without physical contact. There is recorded evidence of Nina Kulagina moving objects when she underwent more than one hundred laboratory controlled sessions. (*Atlas of the Supernatural, p61*)

At the family circle, in which Tom sat in the 1940s and '50s, this happened frequently in the dark, and I have

also known it happen when we had a home circle in our home in Brayton near Selby, in 1998-99. On some occasions, it was the same Crinoline-lady bell, as used fifty years before, which was picked up and shaken over our heads. But also notepads and a plastic garden chair were transported across the room. On one occasion, an envelope containing a card was

*The orginal Crinoline-lady bell, weighing 22oz(600gm).*

brought into the room from the hallway through a closed door, hitting my shoulder as it fell. That, therefore, was an apport, as well as telekinesis. On this occasion, we also had spirit writing, for the Guide had added his initials to the envelope. The card was a farewell message to us, and our names were written in ballpoint on the envelope, but the Guide had added his initials in pencil! After almost fifteen years the Ballpoint has faded and is unreadable, but the pencil of the Guide is as clear as ever.

*The Guide's initials GW are as clear as ever but the ballpoint above has faded.*

One of the first happenings of this kind, after Tom's passing, was not a movement of an object but the movement of a switch.

Here is what I wrote at the time:

*December 25th, 2010:* My 70th Birthday. 6.20am

As I woke I distinctly heard Tom say "Cheese," as though for a photo.

Sleepily, I went through to the kitchen to make a cup of tea and switched on the bank of sockets by the kettle to switch on the power. The power light came on, but the table lamp on the end of the mantelshelf, which is plugged into this bank, did not light up as it always does. (Our lounge has no direct daylight so we, invariably, kept lit all day.)

I thought that the low-energy bulb must have burnt out. I took it out, but then thought I would try it in another lamp – it lit. I put it back into the lamp and started to try the switches and the plug. No success with the rocker-switch, set mid-way along the wire. This was how we would, usually, switch it off and on. I tried moving the plug to another socket – nothing. Then something made me try the switch at the top of the lamp base, immediately below the bulb. The light came on!

We never used that switch, because it meant reaching across the chair and up under the lampshade – very awkward. At night, the lamp was always switched off by switching off the bank of sockets.

Now that is 'phenomena' – a lovely birthday present.

I cannot say that Tom did it, but I do know that the intention of my family in spirit was to give me 'a present', and show me how close they were for my 'special' day.

One other strange happening which I have tried to replicate, unsuccessfully, involved the movement of Tom's pillow on the bed.

Following the loss of a much-loved partner, I am sure many of you have snuggled down to sleep imagining that they are still there beside you. Early in December 2011, a year after Tom's passing, I had been changing the pillows around. I had put the thinner 'under' pillow, that Tom had always used, under my top pillow, so I could lie a little flatter, and put my plumper one on his side under the top pillow, making it higher than he would have liked. As I said 'Good night' I commented that I hoped the pillows weren't too high for him.

When I woke the next morning the top pillow at his side was not on the bed. It was standing upright, neatly on end, between the bed and a bedside cabinet. Yes, you say, I had

pushed it out in the night. Having taken this photo I put it back on the bed and lay down beside it, in my normal position and tried pushing it out.

The distance from the bed to the cabinet meant that the pillow wedged itself against the bedside lamp. Its plumpness would not allow it to bend on to the floor.

Was this an answer? The pillows were too high or just confirming he was around – anyhow, for me it was a happy start to the day.

I described earlier about the crystal swan being moved, but in January 2012, during the home circle, Barbara told

*The frame's usual position.*

*How I found it after Barbara's message.*

me that she had seen Tom holding a photo frame with a picture of the two of us. She even knew the colour of his shirt (not the blue one this time), and he had told her that he didn't think he had put the frame back in the same place.

That evening when I returned home I went straight to the shelf and found that indeed, the frame was at a completely different angle, as you will see from the photographs opposite.

Two weeks later I made myself a kedgeree. I usually have spinach with it. Having prepared the kedgeree, I went to the freezer to get the spinach cubes to put in the microwave. I like nutmeg on my spinach and when I returned from the next room with the frozen spinach, I found the nutmeg grater had been moved from its pot (the front dumpy one) on the left to the worktop – ready for use. As I have only a small working area, I would not dream of getting the grater out before the spinach was ready. But there it was, beside the hob and ready for use when I walked back into the kitchen! – Just another way of Tom showing he was with me?

*The nutmeg grater had been moved from its light-coloured pot on the left of the picture to the right of the hob, ready for use.*

I have had no *verbal* proof from a medium that it was him, but the Acacia Circle was at that time experimenting with table movement. On the following evening, when we knew Tom was present at the circle, I asked if he had moved the grater. We got a very enthusiastic rocking of the table, confirming this. I also felt a strong breath on my neck during the sitting. This could not have been from one of the other sitters. He was close by as he loved the table sittings.

In June 2012, during the visit to Ray Bailey, a good friend who is a medium, Tom drew very close and so, as I have already told you, and we had an impromptu sitting lasting over one hour. Ray told me of the presence of a child, a relative of Tom's, who had grown up in spirit and who was now teaching him how to do things.

*Susan, aged 10.*

Tom's granddaughter Susan passed in 1981, when she was just ten years old, and he told her story in his book. Particular to that story was the movement and disappearance of fruit after her passing – so is Susan showing him how to move objects? I am frequently told by mediums that a young girl is with him and showing him how to do things! Gay too had told us she has grown prettier, and when she comes to me I see her with long wavy brown hair.

In the autumn of 2012, I decided to convert the cassette tapes of some music I love to CDs. As each one was finished, I tried it out on the small hi-fi unit on the dresser. This works best with a remote control as the buttons on the unit are fiddly. One afternoon, when I went to switch it on, the remote control was nowhere to be found. Where had I put it? I searched in all the usual places and then the unusual places, drawers and cupboards – still no sign of it.

Eventually, I gave up, and I went on to do other work. Weeks passed and occasionally I would search again. Then one day, about two months later, I needed some lined paper and saw a pad in the stack of filing trays beside Tom's desk. These were still full of his old papers. As I pulled the pad out there was the 'remote', towards the back, hidden by the wooden shelf fixed above the filing trays. I would never have put it in there. It had been well hidden!

In late November, during one of our mediumship development group sessions, Paul, one of the trainee mediums at the centre, had given me a message from spirit that I had to clear out all the rubbish – get rid! Of course, I did nothing about it. I'm too busy getting on with new stuff! Perhaps if I had had that clear out, the remote control would have been found sooner. – It has been done now!

I also have the lights flicking off and on, particularly if I'm working very late in the office, but a friend of mine, a clinical psychiatrist in New York USA, had a response from the radio and TV in his daughter's home. This is what he wrote in July 2012:

> I had my baby grandchild sleeping on my chest – we both were very tired. I am worried about the health of my son-in-law and the stress on my daughter. A song came on the radio which reminded me of my mother. I said (to myself), "Are you here, watching over them? If so, please, send a sign." Moments later, the radio turned itself off, and the television turned itself on! No one was in the room but me, my wife and my grand-daughter. My daughter and son-in-law were shopping. When they came back, I asked if that ever happened before. They said no. You would have to use the remote or manual controls, neither of which we had touched, and there was no power surge, because nothing else was affected.

And the 'happenings' are still continuing. One morning recently (September 2014) as I was preparing the fruit for my breakfast I reached out to the same pot as holds the nutmeg grater, for the peeler, to find it wasn't there.

Strange, I thought. I had put all the cutlery away an hour earlier, when I was feeding the cat.

Surely I hadn't put it in the drawer. No, it was not there.

I turned back to the drainer, it wasn't there either. Turning back to my bowl, by the hob, the peeler was perched on the edge of the work surface in front of the hob – right where my left hand would be to use it.

I am not going blind, nor, I hope, am I losing my marbles. I would definitely not have put it in such an awkward position, one inch from the edge of the worktop. I feel Tom was announcing his presence as it was the first morning that our circle would be sitting, after a long summer break. He was ready and showing he was with me.

Little things mean a lot!

*Eighteen*

# The 'Clairs' – connections through the mind

Much of our information is perceived mentally – that, for me, much of the time is telepathically – mind to mind. Some people dispute that it is always so, and I have to agree, as when we link psychometrically, we pick up vibrations from the object, which can be remarkably accurate.

We pick up pictures, sensations and feelings from – who knows where? We are often unaware to what we are connecting, because we do not appreciate what our minds are capable of.

During my mediumship development, a tutor said to me "But where do you think it is coming from?" I had to say "I don't know." I may not have been aware of a spirit guide or communicator passing information to me, but what I did know, was that it was not sensed from the person sitting in front of me (which would have been a psychic perception), but it was correct.

There are said to be four primary channels of mediumship, clairsensing (mental), trance, healing and physical, plus a whole raft of others that do not fit neatly into any one primary channel.

Clairvoyance has come to be the term attached to all forms of psychic perception, but clairvoyance (seeing a mental picture) and clairaudience (mentally hearing words) are both really a kind of clairsensing and usually referred to as 'mental mediumship'. Many mediums who are good clairvoyants may well have little or no clairaudient capability and vice versa, even though both 'gifts' belong in the primary channel of 'clairsensing'.

I suppose, if we consider our physical senses, we have sight, hearing, touch, feeling, taste and smell, and each of these can be receptive to impressions beyond our everyday physical range. So 'clairsensing' is a good term to encompass all of them.

However, there is also clairsentience, usually used to describe other feelings a medium may experience such as:

♦ an emotion;
♦ the physical build of a person;
♦ the personality;
♦ an illness the spirit person had
♦ or the medium may, often unknowingly, perform a movement characteristic of their communicator.

Tom often didn't see or hear, he just knew things and I've heard people call this 'clairknowing'. Recently a Spanish acquaintance wrote – "why not 'claircognizance'?" I would second that.

It is a good expression for the certainty that what you are saying or doing is correct, whether it comes as telepathy from spirit, or a knowing from within yourself. As some say – from your higher-self, or even from your soul.

One memorable evening in the late1990s, as Tom and I sat in the lounge at my home in Swanland, East Yorkshire we smelled a strange acrid smell. I could not identify it but Tom could, having been in the army for seven years, during the war. The smell of carbide was well-known to him – gun-smoke. We had not thought about it, but it was near to 11th November – Remembrance Day. His father and William Earle, the young man after whom Tom was named, had both been in the First World War, as had my Uncle Harry.

We did not ask which of them had sent the smell but remembered them all, and it was gone – a memory link from friends and family.

In the Spring of 2012, Kate told me to expect scents, as Tom had learned how to do this. One evening, a short time later, while working late in the office I could smell the strong perfume of Jasmine, which would normally come from the scented 'wax beads' of an American candle 'tart'– although I was at least 15 feet (5 metres) away and they no longer smelled strongly.

A year earlier, I had bought one called 'Midnight Jasmine' which I particularly liked, but the smell had faded away. That evening I was overwhelmed by the perfume. Imagination? I think not – nor was it a warm evening when it would naturally be vapourising. They even give the psychic perception of odours a name now – 'clairaliance'.


When I do link with the spirit world around us. I do usually link via clairvoyance, sometimes not as strongly as I would like to. This is often the way I initially work when I demonstrate proof of survival at a Spiritualist service. At various times, to make the link, I have seen cats, dogs, goldfish, elephants, snakes, someone's favourite toy or book, as well as people and places. But the most special link for me, one morning, as I opened my eyes drowsily, was to be aware of Tom standing beside the bed.

Here is the account of it from my diary:

*December 31st, 2010:* I was up at 5.45am for a cup of tea and an hour later I went back to bed. I kept my dressing-gown on as I was cold. I fell asleep on my back – most unusual – and I was woken, probably around 8.30am, by the most gentle kiss on the lips, that was sensed rather than physically felt. There was Tom smiling, wearing the blue and white M&S summer shirt he wore for special occasions. Then he was gone. I believe I only saw him clairvoyantly but very clearly – looking well and filled out – not gaunt, as he had become. (Barbara has also seen him in this shirt when he has spoken to her.)

Only, very infrequently, have I heard a voice speaking to me from, apparently, within or close to my head. However, since Tom passed I believe they have been working on this side of the mediumship or at least experimenting with it. It usually only happens as I am waking, or I am woken by it, so I must be in a special altered state of mind. I have kept a diary and the range of sounds is ludicrous to say the least. I can, with certainty, say that they are sounds unlike anything which is in my house or surroundings.

Just three weeks after Tom's passing, very early one morning, I heard a man's voice, with a strong Spanish accent, – not Tom's voice – saying 'Olé!' quite loudly. – It was not part of a dream but it certainly startled me.

A week later, I was woken by the sound, coming from the far side of the bed (Tom's side), of a metal pipe being struck so heavily that it rang. I was facing away from it. There is nothing on the table nor in the corner, and nothing had fallen in the office or lounge. Nothing could have made that sound, and no work was being done outside. It was still dark.

The following week at 7.15am a beep-beep sound – as though from the horn on a child's car came from the same area as before, by Tom's bedside cabinet. It took me a few seconds to realise that I had heard it. There is no alarm clock there, nor any instrument that might beep.

In the middle of the month I was woken by Tom saying "plastic roller blind" – very clearly his voice – but for what reason? It had nothing to do with a dream and we don't have one in the house so perhaps that was the reason. It had nothing to do with anything, so it wouldn't be in my mind to be thinking of one and imagine it. Just a pure clairaudience 'test piece'!

*December 23rd:* 7am (2 months now). I heard, from Tom's side of the bedroom, the sound like a thin metal container 'popping'. The sort of sound you usually associate with plastic bottles which as they warm up 'ping' back into shape but this had a metallic tone to it.

*December 25th:* I have already mentioned I heard him say "Cheese."

*January 3rd:* 5.45am I was woken by a very loud noise as though a spring had broken loose in the mattress – a 'bongyyg' sound. The mattress is only one year old and nothing appears to be wrong with it.

*February 18th:* The sounds still continue. This morning, when I had to take the car to the garage for 9.30am, I heard a ping-ping noise around 7.15am; then a gentle 'crack' on the chest some minutes later; followed by a strong 'CLUNK' at the side of me at 7.45am. The garage is only ten minutes away, but Tom always liked to give himself plenty of time!

*February 21st:* 7.15am (again) – that was when Tom would bring me my cup of tea, I heard the honk-honk of a small horn with the rubber bulb – nothing like a telephone or computer. In fact nothing like anything in the house.

*March 6th:* Kate, Marie and Greta, were in Torrevieja on their first visit to Spain. I was to pick them up at 9am to take them to the Acacia Centre for the Sunday service. Fifteen minutes before my alarm was due to go off I heard Tom say from behind me "It's now time." And yes I did need those extra fifteen minutes to find the street in a part of Torrevieja, which was unfamiliar to me.

*April 25th:* 7.15 am. A sound woke me, again behind me, from Tom's side of the bed – a grating clink as though a lid had been put back heavily on a Wedgewood jasperware box, but quite loud – and there are no pieces of Wedgewood at that side of the room.

*November 14th:* I was woken at 7.30am by Tom saying, clearly and quietly, "Are you ready for breakfast?" close to my side of the bed – I answered, "Yes please." It isn't something he would usually have said, but I had to be up quite early as the men were coming at 8.30am to fit my new mosquito screen at the back door, and I hadn't set the alarm.

*November 15th:* 7.55am I heard a distinct 'ding-ding' but of a pitch and sequence unlike anything in my house.

*November 20th:* Woken at 6.30am by a loud 'raspberry' from the wall behind my head. I had a good chuckle and went back to sleep until 8.03 when I heard a distinct 'ding' from the region of the chest of drawers at the foot of the bed. It was far louder and completely unlike Tom's watch timer which is in one of the drawers, but not set for 8am – and again unlike anything else in the house.

*January 26th, 2012:* The twelfth anniversary of moving to Spain. I was woken by the sound of my bedside cabinet being dragged across the tiled floor and then dropped back into place. This was followed by light footsteps at the end of the bed! The cabinet did not look to have moved, but it was a very definite sound – Was it a reminder of our move?

So it continues, but not as frequently. I am not attributing them all to Tom, but it is unlike anything I have experienced before. Nor did we have them before Tom's passing. Occasionally we would hear cracking sounds as furniture expanded or contracted with the heat, but not the same frequency nor range as the sounds I hear now.

In early August 2013 I woke to a definite knock on the bedside cabinet only inches from my head. No, not a clunk or a crack as though the cabinet was expanding – a definite knock-on-wood knock and when I said "I heard that." I had another, lighter knock, in reply. Are they physical sounds? I don't know, they sound as though they are, but there is no one else here to hear them and if it is clairaudience, I hope it continues to develop.

Sometimes I wonder if spoken sounds received in a medium's clairaudience are as clear as we would wish, particularly with names, and perhaps a hiccup can cause confusion in a message, as this one almost had done.

One Sunday morning towards the end of that first year, a medium who is clairaudient, gave me some good evidence, reminding me of Tom's love of Vera Lynn's songs and one in particular *We'll meet again*. He told me, Tom was still with the man who smoked a pipe, and then continued with "You have been trying to mend something, but it wasn't working. You didn't know whether to throw it away or start again." Finally, he said "He is with Derek."

The man with the pipe is my first husband, and I have been told a number of times Tom and he are often together and there is no problem between them. Mending something? My favourite heart-shaped plastic tray from South Africa had developed plastic fatigue and broken. I had been trying, unsuccessfully, to glue it together so, reluctantly, I had thrown it away! – but what did he mean by 'he is with Derek'?

I was worried as to why he was with Derek. Did he mean Derek was with him in the spirit world, or was ill and needed healing? Immediately after the service, I telephoned our friend Derek, who had been unwell. I was relieved to find he was now much improved. We had a good chat, but later that day I had an email from *Eric's* daughter, telling me that he had been admitted to York hospital suffering with severe clinical depression. – Of course Tom would be with Eric, his close friend, with whom we had done so much healing in the past. – Did the medium mishear the name, or was I meant to get in touch with Derek? May be he did need that contact from me. I know we enjoyed our chat.

We have to remember that communication in spirit is by thought, not usually by physical voice so transmitting accurate sounds could be a problem.

A note in Mike Tymn's article *Difficulties in Spirit Communication Explained by Dr James Hyslop* taken from the writings of Rev Charles Drayton Thomas explains the difficulty in getting names through, even when working with a first rate medium in trance (in this case Mrs Osbourne Leonard and her spirit communicator Feda). I quote:

> Etta (Thomas' sister) explained to her brother that it was much easier to send ideas to Feda than it was to send words. She said that she could not get her husband's name, Whitfield, through Feda. "Is it not strange that I cannot say my husband's name?" she communicated. "I can feel it, but cannot say it; that is, I cannot get it spoken. I get it on the surface, so to speak, but cannot get it into the medium's mind." At a sitting four months later, Etta again attempted to get her husband's name through, but only succeeded in getting the medium to say, "Wh--, Whi---, Wht--."
>
> Etta further told her brother that the more she tried to think on the name, the more difficult it was to get it through the medium's brain, adding that she could not control the medium's power of expression.
>
> (Thomas, *Life Beyond Death with Evidence*)

So how much more difficult it must be when the medium is only in a very lightly altered state of consciousness. Maybe, because of that difficulty, that is why the American medium John Edwards, when we see him on television shows, often only gets the first letter of a name.

As for clairsentience, I have already told you how, by the sharp pain in the back of my head, in the exact spot where he had struck his head, I knew when Tom was near. Then once, when writing to a friend and telling her I knew he was near as I had the head pain again, the pain stopped and suddenly a strange fizzing sensation replaced it. I suppose, I could liken it to a light pins-and-needles effect, but less painful. Tom must have been tuned-in, and not wanting me to feel pain or discomfort, had learned to modify the sensation.

It continued like that for some months, whenever he was near, but now there is more a feeling of someone gently ruffling my hair in one particular place.

One of the most physical sensations of his presence was while I was watching the TV programme *Heartbeat* one evening. At a particularly romantic moment I put out my hand along the settee to where he would have been sitting, to take his hand, and instantly it was icy cold, – a sensation frequently felt in a physical séance when a spirit entity draws near. My hand continued to be cold for some seconds as I enjoyed the contact. When I finally asked him to let go of my hand, it was immediately warm again. I had not wanted to break the contact, but I did want to test the result.

Around the same time, I had given Barbara some boxes of the special indigestion tablets which Tom used. We always kept a good stock in and these were still well within the use-by date. Barbara had never had them before so as she was tidying one afternoon she decided to check them out. She wanted to make sure they would not be chalky and she would like them when she got indigestion. During the circle sitting that evening, Barbara felt the presence of someone who suffered from severe indigestion. She didn't know who it was, but she knew the indigestion only came with pastry – particularly puff pastry – but, she asked, would they please take the indigestion away now! Yes, I told her, I could understand that. Tom then made his presence known to her. Tom used to have dreadful indigestion if he ate sausage rolls or apple pie in the evening. Before he learned not to eat pastry late, and discovered those tablets, during the night he would start to cough with the bile – usually 2am! This meant I would have to get up, and mix my special essential oil remedy with honey to stop it – so that, as I told him, I could get some sleep, but more importantly that he did too!!

There were also those occasions, not unlike the one Louie Harris describes in her story about her husband Alec, when some weeks after his death she felt him lie beside her on her bed with his arm across her.

For me, the first time was the morning of my second Christmas. As I woke, feeling so comfortable, lying on my side I snuggled down for a few more minutes. Within moments, I became aware of a strong pressure all down my back and suddenly, I was very hot. There could be no other explanation than that Tom was there. He always was my hot-water-bottle. After a few minutes, the pressure was gone and I was no longer hot, but the peace I felt was beautiful.

I had been given advance notice that something would happen, but had dismissed the thought. The first time was in November, in a trance workshop during Scott Milligan's seminar at the Acacia Centre. One of the students told me to keep Tom's side of the bed clear as he would lie beside me and I would feel him there. Then on Christmas Eve, I had an email from Kate telling me that Aunt Agg was telling her that I would feel Tom's presence and it was my 'stocking present'. This second 'treat' I thought would be the usual ruffling of the hair, so it was lovely to have the special 'presence' present.

Incidentally I did feel my hair being ruffled, a number of times, in the next few days.

Four months later at the end of April, I again experienced the pressure on my back as I woke to the familiar sigh he used to make as he cuddled in.

I do not need these contacts as proof of survival but more as a support system for me that, although unseen, my dear man is still near. I know it is not just for me, but Tom also – for, as he said in the September, eleven months after his passing – he is 'missing me'.

I am sure I am not hallucinating nor deluding myself and I know that many of you, whether you consider yourself mediumistic or not, have experienced similar sensations in like circumstances.

*Tom, the Great-Grandfather, with his great-granddaughter and her brother, his latest great-grandson (2005).*

*Nineteen*

# Connections to build a circle

During the Stewart Alexander and Friends seminar at Cober Hill in October 2011, I felt strongly that I wanted one of the attendees to meet Kate, as they live only a few miles apart. Annemarie, as already described, had helped Tom through his transition, and a few months later Kate had been shown the vision of the same submarine-shaped pod as Annemarie. It appeared to me they were definitely linked and she would make a good sitter for Kate's circle. I am sure Tom was pushing me to make this connection, it felt so right.

It was a couple of weeks before they could meet up, but this is what happened.

> Monday, November 14, 2011 10:11am.
>
> Hi Ann, greetings from Annemarie, Fleetwood.
>
> Many thanks for your connection to Kate. I hope she won't mind me connecting with her.
>
> I feel sure that there is a reason for this. My hands were fair buzzing yesterday when I was linking into Spirit. I felt a sudden thrill in the atmosphere with the words being sensed rather than spoken, 'let's get the party started.'
>
> Annemarie.

Annemarie told me she wanted to send a card to Kate and had felt drawn to get out one of the humorous cat cards. They had been in the cupboard for some considerable time, but here was exactly what she needed, and felt Tom strongly behind the thought.

When she received it, Kate felt this was Tom's way letting her know that this was what he wanted to try.

This is what she wrote:

Wednesday, November 16, 2011 1:18pm

Alloa Ann x

I received a card from Annemarie yesterday - would you believe, it is a TOM cat sunning himself on what looks like a

Mediterranean beach! The cat is wearing glasses, which make his eyes look large, to which I was immediately drawn, reminding me of how large Tom's eyes were behind his glasses. Anyway I rang her this morning and we are to meet in the little cafe in Carleton next Tuesday morning – so looking forward to this and thank you for the introduction.

Kate

In my reply to Annemarie, I explained that Kate had not seen Tom for some years when he had worn large framed glasses. I attached this photo of him, complete with a large grin and wished them luck for their 'get together'.

*Tom in 1998*

They hit it off most congenially and plans were made for the circle.

On the final morning of that same seminar in October, the place at the breakfast table I had had all weekend had been taken so I moved to another table, and asked if I might join them. During the meal, the young woman seated next to me asked if she might have the address of my friend in Blackpool (Kate), whom I had mentioned in the talk the previous day. As she lived in the Blackpool area, she would rather like to have a sitting with her. Out of the blue, I found myself telling her that I thought that she might make an excellent addition to Kate's circle as I believed she was looking for sitters. I then discovered she was Martine, the niece of Violet from Australia, who had the table 'flying' experience. Was Tom at work again – I believe so.

At the time I was impressed to put them all in touch, Kate had linked up with another group and thought there was no need – or rather no space, for more sitters. Some of her new sitters had been part of a trance circle for a good number of years but had never experienced physical mediumship before. Over the weeks Kate tried, to no avail, to explain to them the response that was needed in her circle.

During one usual Friday sitting Aunt Agg came close and impressed Kate that she was going to walk round the circle and touch everyone and they would feel it physically. Kate did not tell anyone, in case it planted a thought. However, the following Friday, as they were having their cup of tea after the circle, one of the sitters said that his hands had been lifted up. Then one by one everyone said they had felt someone touch them on their hands. Kate told them that Tom's Aunt Agg had told her previously that she was going to try to do it. Now at last they were beginning to realise the differences between the trance circle they were used to and her physical mediumship. But cracks were beginning to appear and Kate, not altogether un-reluctantly, disbanded the circle. Now was the time for the people to whom I had been drawn to come together and they all connected well.

Martine proved to be a good sitter in Kate's circle, and as the new circle developed it became apparent that the Saturday Night Club of the 1940s/50s was working with them to try to achieve physical phenomena in the 21st century and Tom frequently made his presence known.

As Tom had formed such a close bond with the team behind Stewart's circle in Hull we thought that would be the group he would continue to work through. But other plans were afoot and in mid-April 2012, once the new sitters had settled in, while we were at the Cober Hill seminar, Kate passed this message on to me:

> He thought he knew everything, well not everything – a lot on this side but he's learning so much on that side. He's got three important teachers his Mum, his Aunt Agg and I've got to put Sunrise in there too. Those are the three main ones that he does link in with. Tosher's taught him such a lot as well in a quiet way. He works – with Tosh – and I've got to say Walter. ["Who's Walter[1]?" *Kate asked, not knowing Stewart's team.*] He knows Walter ... and he's in a group of people that he is privileged to be in because it's his Mum and his family's connection, but he knows the privilege of being in that group to learn from, and he's passed his exams ... flying colours 'cos he's had good tuition. He is acknowledging his teachers. He's going to come through again with me on this voice box (*Kate points to her throat*). He's not leaving me out, bless him, cos we've had that link. We've got this link, so again it is easy.

---

1. Walter is Walter Stinson, one of Stewart's main communicators and the moving force behind the physical manifestations in Stewart's circle. Walter was the main spirit control behind the work of his sister, 'Margery the Medium' in 1920s USA.

The following week, sitting in Kate's home, Tom had more to pass on through Kate's amazingly close connection.—

He loves the connection [we have] here, he loves the connection we had with Cober. He was part of the triangle.

He's met my Gran and he likes her. They have a lot in common and the more he knows my people, the more he can come in this way, (*Her voice started to break and became hoarse.*) on this vibration, 'cos it's his [new] knowledge on how to communicate with different mediums. That's the skill. [*That's what he had said to me a few weeks before.*] It's not who you know, it's not the person – it's how to come through the energy, the vibration and the people that are around the medium as well. That's the skill that he has to learn and he is learning. So by getting to know my Gran it's beneficial for him to be able to use this (*again pointing to her throat*) as a bit of extra proof. He's coming in strong now. He never thought he could, because coming through physically, as you know, has more impact than mental mediumship (Ann. Absolutely, yes.) and when he can speak and build which he is going to try his best – to build – then he's cracked it, he's done it and it will get easier and easier to do it.

He's taking me back to the attic because that's why and when it started – the links. It started then without him knowing his preparation. (*Kate started to feel uncomfortably hot.*) – My back is boiling, but only half my back – down one side 'cos my Gran has given him the link and shown him how to do it … but the sitting in the attic was the energy, the link for this … without him knowing he had to go to spirit to understand himself why the link was forged.

When Kate first started her home circle the only space she could devote to it was the attic of her terrace house. She later wrote to Tom, with a question about the circle, and in his reply he asked if there might be space for two more chairs in the attic. There was, and our friendship developed.

We cannot begin to appreciate how far ahead events are planned in the spirit world, to be able to get the required network of connections for our spiritual work – that a few words spoken at the end of a talk on Physical Mediumship would lead to this collaboration sixteen years later.

Tom's connection with Kate continued to develop and during a phone conversation with me in July 2013, as she was telling me "I've got a man here that you know very well and he's got a Cheshire cat grin." She was so strongly overshadowed that he was able to speak to me direct:

> I can come through Kate so easily, (Ann. You can.) easily and this is better than any phone call on earth to earth 'cos it is spirit to spirit. (A. Darling! ) You can feel it? (A. I can!) And I can come through so you can actually feel it. (A. Yes, I can.) I am always with you. (A. I know you are, so close.) All my love.

Kate told me, because she was not in full trance, she could feel his mouth on hers and although she was speaking – it was him speaking. He was so strong. A powerful overshadowing that, with her Gran's care from spirit, she is happy to let happen. That afternoon he also affirmed for her a connection to a local wartime pilot, of whom she had previously been aware, and who Tom had been helping to make contact with the circle.

For eighteen months the Kate, Annemarie and Martine sat each week with a good rapport between them and, when her business commitments didn't taken her abroad, Kate's daughter, Jo also joined them.

However, as so often happens, and our lives change, there were again changes in the circle. Annemarie had, for personal reasons, to withdraw and a close friend of Martine's joined the circle. With a beautiful balance of energies, the work now continues to move steadily forward, with Tom and the rest of the Saturday Night Club working with them.

*Twenty*

# Physical mediumship connections

In early November 2011, Scott Milligan, a young physical medium, came to the Acacia Centre in Spain for a long weekend to take workshops on trance. Our connection with Scott however, went back to July 2004 when, after a dinner with David Thompson and his circle, a very young man asked if Tom and I would sit for him in his physical development circle. We were delighted to accept, particularly as his development was being overseen by John Austin in Hove.

The friendship between Tom and John went back many years to when John had been advised by someone at the Arthur Findlay College to contact Tom. He was having difficulties with his Home Circle and they said Tom was the best person to help.

When John rang and explained the problem, Tom told him – 'disband the circle and in a few weeks you will start a new one as someone will come to you.' Now although Tom shied away from mediumship and he loved to give healing – just occasionally he was inspired to say something and this was one of those times.

The young man who became the focus of the new circle actually came to lay a new carpet, and asked if John held séances in that room. He could sense it as he was already a good mental medium. John formed a circle around him, and that young man went on to great things in physical mediumship. Years later he returned to his mental mediumship work and was featured on TV.

One of this medium's home circle sitters was young Scott, who started sitting with him at the age of seventeen, but he too had great potential within his own mediumship.

He had already begun his development with John so we were delighted to have the chance to sit. What a circle that night! As well as the usual sitters and John, the circle leader, we were joined by David Thompson and his wife Bianca (shortly before they left for Australia). The entry in my diary for that year says, 'A Good Night!'

*A Circle at John Austin's home. August 2004.*
*Scott standing 2nd left, David Thompson (with mug in hand),*
*Tom standing to right with John sitting in front of him.*

At the Acacia Centre I was now to see how this young man had developed.

Early in his introductory talk Scott told us he had once asked his mentor, John, what a spiritual person was like, and John had told him to look at Tom Harrison.

Tom would not have considered himself such but besides being very human and down to earth that was the effect he had on many people.

Besides encouraging those attending the weekend to develop their trance state, we were to see the phenomena created through Scott's own physical mediumship.

In the séance on the Saturday evening we witnessed many different types of phenomena including, in red light, seeing streams of ectoplasm coming from him and hearing voices speaking through a voice box away from the medium. Towards the end of the séance, when the voice box had been operating for some time, Daniel, the child guide of the circle, speaking from the centre of the room, several metres from Scott in the cabinet, said, "I don't usually do this but the voice box has dried up and so I will try to relay what they want to say." The person wasn't named nor to whom they wanted to speak, but Daniel said:

– Someone keeps picking up a photo and wiping their hand across it and putting it down.

*No one else spoke up so I accepted it! – Tom had said he would always be there.*

A: Yes. – (*It was almost right, more usually it is the picture of him that comes up on the computer screen.*)

D: You still have a tie, a most colourful one.

A: Yes. – (*the wedding tie*)

D: His mother met him. You stroked his forehead and said 'I will always love you' after he had passed. He saw you, he was there. (A: Yes.) You need to live for you both now. To continue the work that you did.

D: He was worried that he might go blind.

A: Yes he was – (*but I didn't realise how worried he was until I recently read his diary for 2009*).

D: Who was it that couldn't tell left from right? (A: Me.)

D: You smell his clothes. (A: Yes.)

D: He gives you a rose. He wants to kiss you and what is this about rubbing noses?

A: We used to – Eskimo style, sometimes when we kissed.

D: He's saying 'Don't take the first offer — you will be fleeced less.' — and there is something about being fleeced or stitched up. He is quite cryptic.

A: Cryptic, Yes. (*The crosswords. But I don't understand the rest — yet, but perhaps the second part is referring to my small travelling fleece under-blankets which are two small ones stitched together, which I have insisted on taking everywhere for many years!*)

D: You are aware of him in the evenings?

A: Especially if I work late.

D: Did he like cheese? (A: Not particularly, but I do.) I can see him going to the cheese counter.

A: Yes — I bought 3 packs at Iceland two days ago.

D: There are some photos of him. He needs you to get out the ones of him when he looked his best and have them made larger.

Later, in Rob and Barbara's lounge Scott asked me if I had been looking at some handwritten cards (Yes.). He could see I had been. He continued for some minutes with more personal bits and told me he was finding Tom easy to communicate with.

Earlier that evening, as we were waiting for Rob to come back with the food from the Indian restaurant Barbara counted out seven sets of knives and forks, while I opened the bottles of wine. When she got to the table she found she has eight sets and said: "No you b..., Tom, you are not having supper with us!" She managed to get seven dinner plates but then had eight side plates! He was determined to show he was with us!

As Gay Nash had said almost a year before — "Thomas will always be here."

A marvellous night — and a wonderful weekend.

Something strange occurred at the end of the séance, that none of us had experienced before. The tiled floor was covered in moisture, like a dew. It was extremely wet and slippery, but the wooden walls of the room and the wooden sides of the cabinet were dry. Daniel had told us the voice box had dried up and couldn't be manipulated but we had all this moisture. – Weird! There is so much we do not understand in physical phenomena.

*Tom, in his 80th year, giving his talk at the SNU's
150th Anniversary Celebrations of the start of Modern
Spiritualism in the Arthur Findlay College, March 1998.*

# Twenty-one

# The third festival of physical mediumship

In February 2012, a third festival of physical mediumship had been arranged for the Acacia Centre. Kai Mügge, the German physical medium, was coming for five days and again we were to be treated to three séances in that time, as well as talks from Kai, Robert and Robin Foy.

Now Tom and Kai never met in the physical world but they had been in email contact fairly regularly on matters of physical mediumship, so here was another of Tom's connections.

It was proposed that tiptology or table movement was to be one of the workshops, so it was decided that we had better make sure that we could get a number of tables moving. For some weeks beforehand, part of the home circle session was devoted to working with a different table each week. To make up the number we needed, I took along the card table which Tom and I had always used for our sittings with the Ouija board.

Towards the end of a detailed message for Tom's daughter, Joyce, on the Sunday, before the start of the Festival, Rob asked me if 'Half a pound of tu'penny rice' meant anything to me. It certainly did. That is a line from *'Pop goes the weasel'*, the Nursery Rhyme that started the séance each week in a wonderful circle in Yorkshire that we had sat in eighteen years before. There, in the early days, we always started by sitting round the large dining table. So regular was that beginning that each week as we switched out the light to start, the cockatiel, in his cage in the corner, would whistle the first notes before falling fast asleep.

Rob then completed the message that day by saying that Tom was telling him he would move the table!

On Tuesday morning, 7th February, fifteen of the final eighteen delegates assembled at the Acacia Centre. As well as a number of regulars at the centre, visitors had flown in from USA, Australia and UK for this third festival. Very few of us were known to Kai and his fiancée Julia before this meeting, nor to each other, but we were quickly to become friends. The morning was taken up with introductions and a time for getting to know each other.

After lunch we were treated to a talk by Robin Foy, one of the organisers, about Leslie Flint, the Direct Voice medium, with whom Robin had sat a number of times.

At 5pm, we gathered for an introductory talk as to what we might expect in the séance which was to follow. Following that introduction Kai left us, and we were frisked before entering the séance room to make sure we were not concealing anything harmful. When we were ready, Robin carried out a strip search of Kai in the main house, before he brought him to the special séance room in the garden of the centre.

At the request of the spirit team, the number of sitters for each séance was restricted to eighteen.

Kai had stressed beforehand that it is most unusual for there to be personal communication in his work as the German sitters, usually, want to see phenomena, not make contact with family and friends. So, for one of the early happenings of that evening to be the materialisation of a man within the horseshoe of sitters was something special. The man was described by the main control of the medium, Professor Hans Bender, as – 'tall, ninety-two when he went and part of the British spiritualist movement'. Who else could it be but Tom, back again in his 'home' centre. We heard his familiar shuffling footsteps as he moved across the room. Hans Bender then went on to say the man wished to touch someone in the circle. Because I was at almost the furthest possible point (approx. 3 metres) from the cabinet, I encouraged him to try to touch Barbara who was nearer. But no, with an extreme effort, I felt a firm tap, unerringly, on both my knees (warm, soft but firm fists) before the energy was pulled back towards the cabinet. A few minutes later, after we had sung again, Hans Bender(HB) came back to say "The man, Thomas, wants to tell that lady that he is very proud of her." HB then said he believed that the man used to be in a circle – so true.

We also had instruments being tapped, shaken and moved. We saw fingers against an illuminated plaque over two metres away from the cabinet, coming at the plaque from different directions – not from the direction of the cabinet. We felt touches – I felt as though an owl's wing had moved across my knees and Barbara felt she had an animal with a long tail on her knee. We had been warned that these ideo-plastic formations can occur – so very different from what we, in UK circles, normally experience. In the latter part of the two-hour séance, in good red light, we watched ectoplasm being pulled from the medium's mouth. We had been told that it would be a sticky substance. It certainly appeared to be. It was adhering to the medium's fingers, but he continued to pull it from his mouth, and to pull it apart with his fingers; showing us the fibrous gossamer-like structure of spiders' web threads in the mass of an unstructured web, like the ones I have seen in my garden in Spain.

Towards the end of this demonstration, the fingers of Kai's right hand appeared to rub together and work the ectoplasm to reveal a tiny Buddha form – an apport which was a gift to the Acacia Centre. Julia told us, when it was handed to her by the entranced Kai, although it had come from this sticky mass, it was dry, hot and clean.

In the Thursday séance, after the trumpet had moved around the room conducting the singing, it rested on Rob's arm and he was told to take hold of it. It played hard to get for a few seconds before letting him hold it and they then had a tug-of-war with it. Rob told us that the pull was extremely strong and the sitter next to him could feel Rob's chair moving with the force of holding it.

We again saw ectoplasm being extracted from the medium in red light and piled up on the floor. Once it had been disconnected from the medium, a hand and arm pushed upwards in it from a pile on the floor. (Yes, we were told, in Kai's mediumship they do disconnect the ectoplasm from its physical source.) Then, after re-forming, we watched a column, about six inches across, grow to head height just within the front of the cabinet. The red light was on it all the time – just as Tom must have seen when his Aunt built for the first time in their circle.

Friday was a day off for our visiting medium, and we had a fun day, exploring the basics of dowsing, followed in the afternoon by table tilting – a method employed by the early spiritualists to communicate with the spirit world. We did not attempt to laboriously spell out the alphabet to communicate, but we, and we assume, the spirit children had lots of fun moving the tables. We had five tables available for the session, and by four of us resting our hands on the top of a table, whilst we sang Nursery Rhymes and other joyful songs. We very quickly had most of them racing around the room and playing 'tag' – stopping within two inches of each other, before shooting back in the opposite direction. The control was amazing!

Towards the end of the afternoon our home circle sitters, plus one other sitter, a medium who was well known to me, sat around our card table. All the other participants sat in a circle around us. We wanted our spirit friends to try to levitate it, but the energy was declining. I started to sing 'Half a pound of tu'penny rice....' – just as I had been told on the Sunday.

Immediately the table became energised and spun wildly around, pirouetting on one leg for some minutes whirling rapidly under our hands as we stayed put, on our chairs. Barbara and I could sense Tom's presence and so could one of the other visiting sitters, who had known him years before, but did not know of his promise for this week.

A wonderful experience.

On Saturday afternoon, we had our third séance. As well as feeling touches, my hair was stroked from behind. We saw hands against a plaque. Instruments were shaken and tapped in time to the music, and then the wonderful experiment which the controls of the medium Rudy Schneider had done many years ago. A handkerchief, with luminous spots on the corners, was plucked, on two occasions, by some form of psychic rod from the outstretched fingers of two different sitters. We then watched it float around the room on the end of this invisible rod, like a jellyfish, even going beyond the circle over my head (I was nearer the cabinet this time).

More personal evidence was given to a sitter, Dr Neal Rzepkowski from the USA. Neal is a medical doctor and one of his patients came back to thank him for all his help in understanding what lay beyond death. A Sioux Indian medicine man, who is a guide of his circle in America, also came bringing him a Peace-pipe and gave the Lakota words "wičháša wakȟaŋ" meaning 'medicine man', which Neal knew. We could hear feet pattering against the tiled floor as HB passed on the information. Neal assured us, later, that he had not mentioned what he did and no one knew the Lakota words and their connection with him.

Louisa, another sitter, was given a contact from a guide who comes to her when she is writing music, which gave her a great boost in confidence.

HB asked for a message to be passed on to 'the lady named Morgana?' He said she was correct and also gave the name of Walter and described the man. Morgana was in fact Morag, a local medium, who could not be there that evening. She had told us that she had felt the presence of her father on the Thursday evening as she wanted to whistle during the singing – a sure sign for her that he was close by. Kai had not been told of this, but HB was confirming that she was correct. Morag later told us the description of the other man was very accurate. It was her husband's uncle – an excellent connection.

Towards the end of the séance the red light, on full 40-watt exposure, again showed us the ectoplasm streaming from Kai's mouth, with him pulling it out. This time it was not sticky and looked like cotton wool flowing across his knees on to the floor and again he pulled it open with his hands to show us the internal gossamer thread structure.

Julia was instructed to turn off the light and then, within seconds, to put it on and it was all gone – reabsorbed, we were told into Kai's etheric body.

HB then asked Julia if she trusted them. Very tentatively she replied, 'Yes.'

'You do not sound sure.'

'I thought you might be asking me a question.'

'Well, do you trust us?'

This time, more firmly, she said, 'Yes, I do.'

At her reply he asked her to get the torch with white light and shine it on to the floor by her feet. She was then to slowly move the light up on to the cabinet and up the curtain. As she did so, we could see Kai's face poking through the opening of the cabinet curtain. From his nose were twisted 'ropes' of ectoplasm which then looped round into a mass of looser ectoplasm, seemingly attached to the cabinet curtain to the medium's right, several inches away from his face. HB asked if we could see a face in the ectoplasm — it was his face, he told us. From my position in the circle, I could not see it as the mass was turned slightly away from my side of the circle but most of the others could. It was held for quite some seconds before Julia was asked to turn the light out.

This must be the first time that white light has been directed on to ectoplasm for many, many years. The light was quite bright too and only approximately two feet (60cms) from the mass. The lamp was the flat sort we used to use as the front light for a bicycle.

These had been amazing séances, so much light and openness.

During the séances, Kai has no straps or restraints securing him to his chair as many other mediums do. This freedom of movement is essential because of the need to pull the ectoplasm from his mouth so that he does not choke.

Whenever movement of objects or the formation of hands was occurring in the room, he was put under the control of Julia and Sandra Foy, who were sitting either side of him. They each placed one hand on the leg nearest to them and held his hands with their other hands. Occasionally Sandra was asked to reach across and check that Julia was still holding him too.

A wonderful five days of variety and contact with spirit!

*Twenty-two*

# Communication through a table

Following the success with the table movement during Kai's week at the Acacia Centre it was decided to do more work with the table in the home circle. As my card-table was light in weight, a good height for us to sit or stand at, and had responded the best during the seminar, it was selected for the circle. It was also a slightly larger surface for six or seven of us to stand or sit around.

It was soon clear that we had an energetic team working with us, and for some weeks at the beginning of our experimental sittings the table soon had us out of our seats and moving – even racing – around the room to much laughter. In response to a request to turn in a different direction when it was spinning it would stop and reverse. It was not long before we decided to stop running around, and let the table slide under our hands as it turned. We quickly established a pattern of working so that we did not leave our seats and the table began to communicate in response to our questions by rocking to make a tap of the legs for yes and stillness for no.

All questions had of course to be phrased so that a yes or no answer could be given. We did not resort to spelling out the alphabet as we had done in that circle in Yorkshire, when I had been known as the 'alphabet lady'. Then, I had asked – before M? – after M? and spelled out the letters, till we arrived at the correct one when the table would twitch in reply – a most laborious exercise!

As the weeks passed, a system developed, more from the spirit side than ours. The table would move close to the person with whom the spirit person wished to communicate. We would then ask if it was a member of the family, a friend or a helper making him or herself known. Although most of the circle sitters were able sense which category the visitor fitted into we never assumed who it might be. If the communicator was for all of us the table would move in towards each of us in turn, as a greeting and then stop in the centre of the group.

The fun started when the spirit team working with us found that they could make different sounds either by the movement of the table legs, tapping on the tiled floor in rocking movements, or grating when pushing it across the tiles.

One evening, having established contact, it was rocking rhythmically so it ticked like a clock which the communicator had left as a gift to her grandson. When he commented that he wouldn't have thought of a clock with her, the table changed rhythm to be that of a horse galloping – yes she did like a bet! Laughter was the order of the evening for these sittings and oh, so much love.

For another sitter, after the table, had pushed itself against her to indicate a connection, a rhythmic sound was created, like snoring. When someone recognised the scraping of the legs as being like snoring, we had a rapid rock, forcefully banging the legs to the floor to say 'YES'. The sitter knew then her uncle was present, as snoring had been given previously, by a medium, as a characteristic of his. The table then moved close to her and gave her what we called a 'hug' by pushing itself into her midriff.

Tom, of course, was not to be left out of this fun means of communication.

*June 7th:* The table moved hard into my midriff. It was Tom. As I spoke to him the table moved heavily against me. When I asked him about visiting Maggie, a medium friend, and telling her about the tree, he responded with a tip to knock 'yes'. It gave a 'yes' again when I asked if had he inspired them at another spiritualist centre to pick one of his stories as the reading, when one of our circle was conducting the Sunday service for them. 'He' (using the table) then went over to her and gave her a 'hug'.

*July 19th:* Very early in the sitting the table went into 'sounds mode' and produced the scraping sound which John P., a communicator speaking through Rob, (who was in deep trance), said was rather like a saw. I asked if it was someone I would know? (My father was a joiner and had made the table we were using). (John P. 'Oh dear!') The sound then became uneven – like a saw used badly. Three days earlier, I had used a rather rusty saw to cut the end of a broom handle, in order to repair it, and I am not good at using a saw. They were telling us that someone was around when I was working. The table then responded by making the sound of hammering – rocking, to bang two legs to the floor, which I'd had to do to get the handle back into the brush head. I don't know whether it was Dad or Tom, but they were showing they are close and watching whatever I get up to.

*August 23rd:* About half-way through our sitting on this particular night, Barbara got a terrific pain on the right side of her head. She felt a soldier beside her. This pain continued for some minutes until she asked me if Tom had a friend in World War I. As she spoke, she was surprised that she said WWI because she had originally thought of WWII. I told her, yes he did – his namesake William. The table rocked to crash down 'YES', loudly. One of the other sitters had also sensed the name William earlier in the sitting. I explained that William was Tom's second name, after a young soldier who was taken under Toshy's wing (Tom's father) when they were in the trenches. The table went mad – rocking back and forth excitedly.

I asked, "Is it Willie? Willie Earle? Really?" The table continued to rock and bang the legs heavily. With that Barbara had a blast of cold air over her and I felt it across my shoulders (It had not been cold before, even from the fan cooling the room).

"Oh Fantastic, Brilliant." I continued, and felt a strong pressure on my head. I told them that I thought it was July 1918 that he had been killed, just before the end of the war, and a very short time before Tom was born.

"It's lovely to have you here. Have you met up with Tom? He'll be so pleased." The table moved again to knock in a 'yes' reply.

Barbara told us that when she thought about it the uniform was from WWI, but she knew Tom was present in the circle and that was the confusion.

*August 30th:* Towards the end of this sitting the energy changed and the table moved to me. Was it Tom? – The table banged against my knee in confirmation.

Barbara asked if he was coming to visit the David Thompson seminar again this year. We had a strong 'YES' in reply. Barbara then mentally picked up information from him and asked me if I had done something with the chair he used to sit in. I told her I had. I had cleaned it and covered it, along with its twin, with the yellow throws from the guest room. The table again nudged into me in acknowledgement.

It then began moving in a figure of eight. Barbara voiced that it was moving like in a dance and there was also a letter S – 'Yes' the table responded. Now, the figure 8 could be Tom's sign, as in their old circle when the trumpet moved in different ways to show who was present, – and his birthday was the '8th of the 8th'.

I immediately knew it was about our Street Party on September 14th. I told them that I had been thinking about this, adding that I found it difficult to go to it since Tom died. The table responded with a very strong 'YES'.

Barbara spoke to Tom "You don't want to miss it do you, Tom?" There was a strong response from the table rocking–rocking–rocking. I told them because every year we had danced at it so much it was still a too emotional memory. There was a strong movement by the table again in agreement. It then pinned Rob in his chair and finally came to me and I promised to get a ticket for the Party.

It was a slightly bittersweet visit to the Street Party, but I thought of him dancing with me as I did manage to do a dance or two with the other ladies there, whose partners weren't dancing.

That was the last of our table sittings in the circle as we moved on to do other work, but it was certainly fun and a good way of communicating.

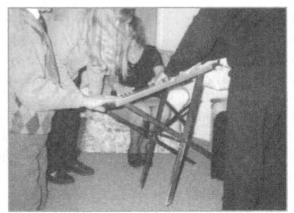

*I haven't a recent photo of communication through a table but this is one taken in our home in Brayton, Yorkshire in 1998.*

*Twenty-three*

# Eastbourne, September 2012

While browsing on the internet for sites about physical mediumship, I came across a notice about a five-day seminar in Eastbourne. There it was going to be possible to sit with four physical mediums – Kai Mügge, Scott Milligan, Bill Meadows and Terry Tasker over the five days. On top of that José Medrado from Brazil was to demonstrate his amazing trance oil-painting. No, it wasn't possible that there would even be a room left by now. I dismissed it, but back and back it came – 'Go on, you can, you can. Try.'

I was put on to a waiting list, happy, eventually, to have any room available. Within an hour, I heard there was a single room. Then, only a few days before I was to go, I heard that a spacious double room with a sea view was to be mine. Although there was not a lot of time for sitting and looking at the view, nor walking on the promenade, the weather was perfect – warm, sunny and calm. Then, to top it all, when I arrived, I found a number of good friends were there and the organisers had put most of us in the same group. How did they know? – Already a good blending of harmonious energy for the coming séances.

Scott Milligan has always said, it doesn't matter where you are sitting, if spirit want to get to you they will. His advice is – always to go into a sitting hoping that the person next to you will get a message – and that will create the harmony for a good séance. I have to admit though, I had said to Tom that I hoped he would make it through at some point. He has been so well-known that it would be a bonus for many people if he could connect with at least one medium. He did!

I have already written how, when Scott came to our 'home' centre in Spain, young Daniel had to pass on Tom's message to me as the voice box had dried-up.

Now ten months later, at Eastbourne in September 2012, Tom was able to use the independent voice box. Quietly, but distinctly towards the end of the séance with Scott we could hear him say 'Annnn...' He then went on to say that he had come as I wished, but it was difficult.

Telling me I was his best girl, he then said he wanted to have the first dance with me – but not for some time! This was a reference to our 'village' Street Party in Spain that I had – rather emotionally – attended the previous Friday, just as he had asked me to (through the table movement).

He went on to say, "You know that dome...."

"Yes, was it you who cracked it?" (*I should know better, I had jumped in too quickly.*)

"That was what I wanted to say. You have no need of bells and whistles."

Unbeknown to Tom, some years before, Rob and Barbara had bought a large glass dome for sittings at the Centre, as used by the Scole Group when they sat in the 1990s. Tom had made it clear he felt things like that were unnecessary and so they had kept it hidden in its box while Tom was sitting there. After he died, they got it out and stood it on the table at the side of the circle to see what might happen. During one sitting, shortly after he had passed, we heard a loud crack and on examination we found a long crack right down one side. We have always wondered if Tom was trying to put an apport under it, as this had happened several times at a circle we had been in, in Yorkshire in the 1990s.

Tom then told me he had done something for me. He had written a message – "I didn't know I could do that. Catch my two kisses." We heard the lip-smacking sound of two kisses.

Tom couldn't hold the communication any longer and young Daniel continued for him. He told me there was some music but he didn't know what it was. (For dancing do you think?)

"Did you rub noses, what a funny thing to do?" – "We did Eskimo style," I replied. – He had also asked me that the previous year in Spain but it didn't matter as no-one else knew and it caused some lovely laughter.

Tom always likes to give some up-to-date evidence, to prove on-going survival, rather than just memories – particularly if it can be something that does not readily come to mind. In this way, if it is not at the forefront of your mind, it can't be a mind-reading trick by the medium.

Daniel then asked if I still had Tom's shoe laces – with knots in. I couldn't remember. There was silence while Daniel asked Tom and he then told me – "They are in a box in the corner."

\* \* \* \* \*

When the lights were put on at the end of the séance, in the top corner of one of the three sheets of A4 paper, which Sue Farrow had initialled before the séance began, was written –

**Tom..... With x alway x x.**

And why *two* kisses blown? – this was the nineteenth Anniversary of the day he first kissed me, on the weekend that we met, and yes, that day, it was two kisses.

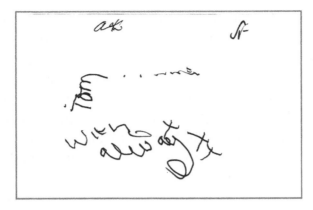

*Tom's message in the top right corner on a sheet of A4 paper,
with, at the top, Sue Farrow's initials written before the séance,
verifying the paper was blank.*

They don't forget the special moments.

This had been a wonderful few days, packed with fun
friendship and contact – a real boost and I managed to buy
a painting by VanGogh, through the hand of Medrado. All
the money raised from these paintings is used to support his
charitable work for the City of Light (Cidade de Luz) which
he founded to help abandoned children in Brazil.

I have had a look for the laces. There are many boxes and
corners around our house, but I have found two pairs of new
laces at the end of a box in Tom's workshop and one pair is
tied in a knot. He always was one for good evidence and
showing he is still around. These were certainly not in my
mind to be a case of psychic mind-reading. I have had so
much evidence about things that are around me but are not
in my mind, that I think he must be constantly searching for
what he can give next – not for *proof* to me but things I can
pass on to you, to show what they are capable of and just
how near they are to us.

# Twenty-four

# A spirit healer makes himself known

I wrote earlier how we met Kate Maesen in 1995, and how that initial meeting led to a close friendship. When Kate confirmed there was space for two more chairs in the attic we happily travelled the forty minutes down the A1 towards Doncaster to be with them once a month.

Later, one of the sitters would bring Kate and another circle member to sit in our home near Selby. It was there, one March evening in 1998, that we heard a sing-song voice say, "Zee shjentleman does not wish to know his new friend." Tom, as often happened, had his eyes closed – providing energy – he said, for whatever phenomena might occur.

Drawing Tom's attention to what was happening, we could see an oriental face in the fine energy mask over Kate's face and the 'new friend' told us he had come to work with Tom, to help when he was giving healing.

Ten days later we were at the Arthur Findlay College at Stansted Hall for Tom to give his talk during the 150th Anniversary of the 'birth' of Modern Spiritualism. One of the well-respected mediums there told Tom she had never heard his talk, and she wasn't going to miss it this time. Tom, in return, told her that he had always wanted a sitting with her and so it was arranged.

When we presented ourselves in her room, she told us that her controlling guide wished her to do a trance sitting (by then, strictly frowned upon by the SNU authorities).

However, because it was Tom she had no concerns about so doing. Within the space of a minute or so she was in trance and her guide was speaking to us, passing on information from the 'new friend', whose name he told us was Ching Lee. Her guide then went on to tell us of the work that was intended. He also explained that his medium had not gone into a 'deep' trance state as she was being 'nosey'. That did not matter to us as the information we were given was good, and confirmed what we had already been told.

Three weeks after that, we went on a second tour of the Bristol and South Wales area, to give Tom's talk at various churches and centres. While there, we called to see one of the ladies with whom we had stayed eighteen months earlier. Somehow during the afternoon the lady who had organised our visit asked our hostess if she still did her drawings. Carol replied she hadn't done any since her father died some years before, but she was persuaded to get out her sketch book and show us her beautiful, detailed work. Kneeling on the floor in front of us, she turned page after page of finely-drawn faces and full-length sketches of the spirit people she had felt close to her. Then she paused and held the pad fully upright in front of us. Tom asked her why she was showing us that one in particular. She replied that she didn't know why.

We told her we did for we could feel the recognition within us – it was Ching Lee. Three times within a month, he had made his presence known, through three very different mediums and the last one as a picture drawn some years before. Carol gladly gave us the picture and it still has pride of place in our Sanctuary.

Over the years, when we were with our friend Eric, he always knew when Tom, or should I say the spirit team, were ready to do some healing on him, as Tom would, unconsciously, try to push his hands up the cuffs of his shirt or jumper – just as in the portrait of Ching Lee, where his hands are tucked well up the wide sleeves of his robe.

Of course, the connection with dear Ching Lee didn't end with Tom's passing into the world of spirit, for now was his chance to teach Tom how to do healing from the spirit side of life.

*Spirit portrait of Ching-Lee*

When Kate and I were sitting together in my home in September 2012, Ching Lee spoke to me through Kate's trance telling me that the three of us were to work together. He would teach me through my mind what to do, for we were a team – Ching Lee, Tom-Tom and Missy-Missy (me). For some time our healing work had been confined to distant healing sessions on Thursday mornings, but in February 2013, at the Acacia Centre, here in south east Spain, a Healing Service was started on a Wednesday afternoon and we were able to be part of it.

In January, before we started the weekly services, I told Robert and Barbara of the rapidly growing cataract in my right eye and the decision of the optician to refer me to a specialist. Rob decided that healing sessions would start immediately – and would probably include psychic surgery. These sessions were carried out in Rob's treatment room with Barbara and two other healers providing extra energy for the work by Rob and the spirit team. On that first occasion, as well as seeing Tom and some of the team of healers and doctors who work with Rob, Barbara was aware of a small Chinese-looking man moving quickly around the healing couch. I had not previously told them of our friend, but he was there when help was needed.

The result of those healing sessions? When I went to a specialist at the beginning of March and again to the optician's, two days later – the cataract had reduced by more than 10 percent. So there was no danger to my sight and my driving licence, and no operation was needed. But what was more, the distance vision in my right eye was now 'normal' – a condition which had not existed for more than twenty years.

The Spanish optician and his English receptionist– although I told them about the healing sessions – put the improvement down to a lessening of my grief over Tom!

Now during our healing services, when I am transferring the energies I can feel Tom on my left and Ching Lee to my right. A wonderful friend and although I feel him close, how I long to meet him in person – in spirit.

How do I know I am not imagining their presence?

One Wednesday afternoon just before the start of the service, a young woman who occasionally comes to the centre moved her chair away from the left side of me as she felt that someone wanted to sit there. She has been aware of spirit presence since a young child, but she did not know it was Tom's custom to be there beside me at this time.

Some people are even aware of their touch. One afternoon as I was directing the energy to one lady's knee, which she said was very painful, she felt fingers digging right into the side of it. She opened her eyes to find that I was not even touching the knee, but she could feel the pressure within it. Without a doubt my friends were there working.

Whenever I visit our friend Eric in York, I always fit in a healing session before I leave him and usually when I am working he can see the spirit team around him. On the last occasion, in April 2014, he was a bit worried, as when he saw Tom he wasn't smiling while I was transferring the healing energy. Eric thought it might mean there was something amiss with his health, but I told him, Tom had, usually, been serious when doing the healing – his customary smiles were for other times.

*Twenty-five*

# "Thomas will always be here."

Over the last two years, Robert has held mediumship development classes at the Acacia Centre and I joined them to help improve the way I worked. From the earliest days, whenever he got the opportunity, Tom was there to help the students, when they had to get a link with someone from spirit to pass on to me. I had some good snippets of memories from him.

Early in the sessions Lynne, to her astonishment, found Tom telling her about painting pictures. She had never met him and although she had read his book, there is nothing in there about that aspect of his life. He loved to paint in oils and watercolours and was very good. I still have several of his watercolours around the house. In the last few years of his life, his painting became much more vibrant but I did not really understand his particular reference to yellow and blue which Lynne gave me, until I returned home.

The plates and bowls we bought when we first arrived in Spain were yellow and blue; the pots for the kitchen utensils were yellow and blue. I had made a new loose cover for a settee in ochre yellow and blue; the blue chairs had yellow cushions. The guest room had covers and curtains in yellow and blue; the bathroom floor used to be covered in a yellow and blue absorbent 'mat'. The small rugs in our bedroom were blue with a yellow design. The symbolic drawing he did linking our initials contained a lot of yellow and blue.

Everywhere I looked around our home there was a mix of yellow and blue. No wonder he had referred to it. It was so much part of our life together.

However, I did not know then, and have only discovered over two years later, what the 'yellow and blue' represents. On arriving at my brother's in October 2014, he made me a cup of tea in a new R.N.L.I. mug he had bought, which depicted the International Code of Signals. I have been fascinated by the flags since looking at the pictures in my father's *Manual of Seamanship* as a young child. Intrigued I examined them and noticed one was yellow and blue, halved vertically. I looked closer. It was the flag for K – Kilo....but the meaning was 'Desire to communicate' – How appropriate and another brilliant cryptic connection!

*RNLI Mug with International Code: K - 'Desire to communicate'*

In late November 2012, during the next session of six weeks training, Paul had an impression of a man who wasn't one for going to churches or was into religion – even perhaps Spiritualism (*That was correct.*) but he felt he had a 'spiritual' man. He hadn't known who Tom was when he saw him at the centre, only as the man who sat in the corner at the back, but he felt that it might be him. He wasn't given a name but could feel a vibrant energy. (*So right.*)

When I asked Paul for some more specific personal memories – which was the purpose of the exercise that Rob had set, – he went on to say that he was being shown something from his own life so he wondered if it was connected. Paul liked to wear socks with sandals – to which his wife objected strongly – and he felt it could be that. (*Yes, for comfort, after a bad spider bite, Tom did wear socks with his sandals.*)

He also saw him walking with a stick which he would wave in front of him. (*Yes, particularly at traffic when crossing the road in Torrevieja.*)

That was good personal evidence which certainly would not have been readily in my mind.

Three days later, Paul was one of the mediums at the 'Fledgling Service' (mediums who are just starting to 'fly'). Again, Tom was there helping and causing a laugh – which is so good for raising the vibrations to help the flow of energy needed for good communication.

This time, Paul was aware of a man close to him but said: "There is something about a light and I feel there was something about a light being left on overnight."

Paul described his communicator's build and added that his passing had been peaceful. "He is going back to the light because that is important – something about the light." I acknowledged the connection.

Paul then addressed the congregation "I'm not particularly getting the relationship, but I have to say I know a bit about Ann and her background. I was sitting with Ann on Thursday and I've got the same feeling, and I think that I may have the same person. (*Ann. You have got the same person.*) I think that I have Tom with me …I do remember Tom being here, though I never spoke to him."

"There's never a dull moment! (*A. No, there isn't!*) He's laughing and I feel there are one or two things that are going on with you at the moment and you think to yourself, 'I can't believe I've just done that.' (*A. That is so right. – [I had been out to dinner that week with a man I had only just met and I firmly turned down the offer of repeat meetings!]*) Thank you. So I'm going to quit while I'm in front. Tom's just sending his love."

Rob explained to everyone the story of Tom and the light in the home circle that I have already related in Chapter 9. So why emphasis on the light now? Just two days before I had gone to bed, very sleepily, leaving the main lights on in the office (3x40watt bulbs) and the lounge (5x25watt though dimmed) *all night*. I had also fallen asleep with the bedside light on. As he said, I could not believe it! It has taken me over two years to get back to sleeping in the almost dark, with only a small night-light and here I had left them <u>all</u> on.

Just before Christmas, Paul heard Tom make reference to a cauldron and interpreted it as someone stirring it up. That morning, I had been asking myself whether I should make my special Christmas puddings this year. This involves a lot of stirring and, as it is quite a different mix with no flour, one might call it a real 'witch's brew' – plus I have to use my largest saucepan – nearly a 'cauldron' – as a mixing bowl.

But why particularly a 'cauldron'? Many people in Spain buy stickers of a bull or daisies to decorate their cars, but I wanted to be different. So when I bought a sticker I told Tom I had chosen a witch on a broomstick, but I'd chosen the one with a handbag!

*My witch with a 'handbag'!*

The sticker (I say it's a car tattoo!) was duly attached to the back of our fire-engine-red Fiesta and a good year passed before Tom came in from washing the car and said "That isn't a handbag! Go and look." I had to agree – it was a cauldron! How daft can you get?

But what a lovely way to bring it back. Again a message with more cryptic fun.

Although Tom had said he preferred working with a feminine energy he did seem to like working with Paul, who in no way could you describe as having a feminine energy. I suppose this was stretching Tom's experience of energies.

In the January-February session of classes, Paul asked if I had lost the remote control for some equipment recently – (*the control for the small music player had turned up just a week earlier – see Chapter 15*). He then continued "He is talking about an itinerary. There is somewhere you are going that is an adventure for you and you have some concern that you will be out of your depth. (*Ann. Yes – [to Norway]*) Don't worry, the Team – you know THE TEAM – they have it all in hand and everything will be all right. They will see it is changed if necessary."

It was changed. A co-incidence? Well – the weather became unsuitable for the proposed extensive driving tour into the mountains and fjords in early May, but I still had a wonderful time with my Norwegian friend.

During that same session, Carol found it difficult to make a connection for me. She felt someone close, but she would not accept it could be Tom. It was too easy to assume that he was there for everyone – so she wasn't seeing anything but an eye – a narrow slit of a bright, twinkly eye – not fully open. As she spoke, she put her hand up to her left eye. I told her that is what I would see each morning when I was trying to put his drops in after the cataract operation. He wouldn't open his left eye fully as he knew the drops were coming.

On other occasions too Carol has been amazed at the strange things she has been given to make a link. Not knowing which of the group to link with, she clairvoyantly saw an acorn. I was the only one who could understand its special significance. She was astounded, as she had not heard about the tree we had grown and then planted in Tom's memory, but contact having been made the evidence given was so accurate.

At a later session, we each had to make a spirit contact for every member of the group. As Carol stood in front of the five of us, she told us she felt like singing the song *Where do I begin* ... Rob informed her that then was her first link. She could hardly believe it when I said it meant something to me. After drawing breath, she told me that she wanted to go on with the rest of the words and to come over and give me a great big hug. – Yes, Tom was with her and the song was like a 'love letter' for me. The rest of the message concerned the writing of this book. When she had finished, I told her how, when puzzling over how to start the first chapter of Tom's book *Life After Death: Living Proof,* I had woken the following morning with that line in my head – a special start to a book about the love of spirit for us all.

In the middle of May 2013, we held a four day *Gateway to Healing* seminar at the Acacia Centre to introduce people to various therapies and healing techniques. Before the start of the final morning Rob heard one of his guides tell him that he wished to speak to the students about healing, and later we were to go into the séance room so they could witness transfiguration in red light, through Rob's physical mediumship. This was the first time that it would have been seen outside the home circle.

Once Rob was in deep trance a number of regular spirit visitors to the circle and some family members of the sitters were seen, in the red light, on the film of energy in front of Rob's face. Then we saw Tom's familiar wide smile and heard his greeting, "Hello, my dear. Hello, everybody."

As he chatted with us, Lynne said, "It's like talking to an old friend though I never met him. I want to thank you, Tom, for all the help you have given me." To which Tom replied

"Well I would have helped you when I was here so why shouldn't I help you now."

Wonderful confirmation of his work with them all.

In the six weeks before our summer break, we had another session of the mediumship development class. At the beginning of the year, I had been told that Tom would not be coming through as often. I would now hear from other members of the family, and I have, but would this include the mediumship development classes?

In the early hours of Thursday 20th June as I woke I heard a woman's voice say – "Tom won't be allowed in there." This puzzled me, but sure enough that afternoon the messages I received were very good but were not from him. Now it was time for the students to connect with other friends and family and learn to work with different energies just as Tom had done with them.

Yes – still 'trivia' but bringing back so many good connections and memories and stretching their experience.

The connections that these developing mediums made over the months were excellent and very often far more meaningful than some mediums we have seen working the churches and centres.

When we started the course of development, all the students were able to see, hear or sense things – so potentially good mediums, able to help others. The skills enhanced during the sessions included learning to use all aspects of their sensitivity – vision, hearing and feeling. Also to be aware of what movements they were making, such as turning a ring on the hand or putting hands together in prayer when this was not one of their usual actions. – Movements like these may often be characteristic of the spirit person, when on earth. They learned to ask for more depth and detail during in a message and to be able to give one contact after another for a required length of time. All this in preparation for a presentation during a service or a private sitting.

At the beginning of July 2013, during my visit to Frederick and Valerie at their villa on the Algarve, Frederick asked if I would take his development group for him while I was there.

'Not coming through' didn't seem to apply to Portugal as two of the three members of the group became aware of Tom's presence. The first lady, who was very new to the group, told me of a young man, tall and slim, in his thirties and with dark hair but later he had glasses. He was happy and he just wanted to let us know he was there, and as she was speaking she could feel that he had a very large energy. It had to be Tom showing himself as he is now – like the picture here when he was thirty.

*Tom ~ 1948*

The second lady, as she held the small gold watch he had bought me, felt the love and the happiness which it carried. She knew it was a present from my husband and then she could see him – "I can see his face, he's smiling. He's actually putting his head back and laughing." Then Tom drew so close that emotion overcame her and tears came to her eyes as she felt the love that he brought.

This group had never met me before and knew nothing of Tom and his work, but that evening he certainly made his presence felt. The rest of us could feel that he was close and of course, he would want to be there with our good friends, Frederick and Valerie.

So like Gay Nash had said to Rob and Barbara, that first December; telling them 'Thomas will always be here.'– he *is* always around! He is helping wherever he can, just as he did on earth, but now he's particularly working to push forward those developing their skills at connecting the two worlds. Through this development and interest more and more people will learn that we continue to live on after death in a wonderful place ... and how we live here *matters.*

---

Thanksgiving

Thank you, God, for the privilege
Of sitting here bathed in your Love,
For having the chance to say 'Thank you'
For the blessings you send from above.

We sit here in the hope of some contact
With someone far wiser than we.
That with their help and their guidance
Greater use in the world we will be.

We send out our peace and our love now,
Thou knowst where best they'll be used,
It may be for nothing dramatic,
Just some help for a soul that's abused.

So we thank you, God, for the privilege,
Of being with those of like mind;
For having the chance to say 'Thank you',
For the wonderful peace that we find.

                                        Ann Ellis

*Twenty-six*

# You only have to ask!

At another Cober Hill gathering, in April 2013, almost two years after Gilly first brought through a reference to a wheelbarrow, the word came back into her head as we chatted together. I told her I had puzzled over this initially, but having seen her notes it all fell into place. So why had it been brought to back into her mind now?

It seemed as though Tom wanted us to realise there was something more to it than a 'cross-correspondence' experiment or demonstrating he was close when I was pruning the lemon tree.

In that moment, I saw in my mind the day in 2001 when we moved from one house, to another in the next street within the 'urbanisation' in Spain. As it was such a short distance, we balanced the large, sturdy plastic garden 'cupboard' (2m tall by 1.5m wide) across a friend's wheelbarrow. With Tom pushing and me steering, we got it round the corners, as far as the entrance to the drive of the new house, but we couldn't manoeuvre it up the slope.

As if by magic, two people belonging to different parts of the urbanisation, but known to us slightly, appeared from different ends of the street and offered their help to get it into place in the garden. Tom had with this single word – and the vision reminded me, not only of a happy memory, but also that help is always near in times of need.

As I told Gilly of this memory we felt that cold shiver of confirmation – the 'someone walking over your grave' feeling – that we had found the right interpretation for this occasion.

Whether it be friends from this world or the other – you are never alone and help is always at hand. Like the afternoon when Tom and I were travelling the ninety miles from Swanland, near Hull, to Darlington to give his talk and we had a puncture on the York bypass. We pulled into the side of the busy A19 just north of York, with a very flat tyre. Getting out of the car, I said to the 'heavens' "We need some help."

As we unloaded all our equipment from the boot, to get at the spare wheel, we heard a voice behind us – "Can I help you, sir?"

There was our 'knight in shining armour'. A six-foot-plus North Yorkshire policeman had stopped to help, on the busy two-way road. Tom asked how he knew we needed help. To which he replied "Ah! The North Yorkshire Police use crystal balls." He didn't realise how apt that remark was!

Protecting us from the traffic with his large patrol car, in no time, he had the wheel changed and we were on our way.

I believe we made a difference to his day too. We were so grateful for his help, that making a note of his number, Tom said he would write to HQ to tell them how helpful he had been, together with a donation to the benevolent fund. As we thanked him, he thanked us too, and told us that he had just had to deal with a speeding female motorist who'd become quite abusive. She wouldn't believe he was a genuine policeman despite the distinctive chequered, 'suped-up' patrol car and his uniform. – "Some people!" was his restrained comment.

An hour later we were guided to a tyre repair place, in Darlington to mend the tyre before we were due to give the talk, and it happened to be just a few yards from our venue.

When you work with love, help is always there. And you can feel very blessed.

Today, as I write a posting came up on my Facebook page:
– Suddenly all my ancestors are behind me.
"Be still" they say, "Watch and listen.
You are the result of the love of thousands."

How True! They are still wanting to look after you, if you will let them, but you do need to ask.

You still have the choice to say – "I did it my way!"

*Twenty-seven*

# Celebration of the third anniversary

Tom always likes to make his presence felt at Stewart's Cober Hill seminars. In October 2012, because of Stewart's health, the phenomena in the séance was less than usual. However, Peter, who senses Tom's energy well, told me later that he felt Tom close by while the trumpet was doing its usual acrobatic flight around the large circle. The trumpet had then paused in its flight and in front of him made the sign of an eight on its side – $\infty$ – the symbol for infinity. He instinctively felt that this sign was showing Tom was near.

I told Peter of the '8' movement we had had through the table two months earlier. Tom had come tonight to let us know it was not 8 but $\infty$. Now, just as the spirit friends in their old circle had their symbols for the trumpet, to show when they were present but not able to speak, he too had his sign. A wonderful piece of communication and confirmation for both Peter and myself.

So, the following October 2013, now three whole years since Tom's passing, he was ready to do something special.

On the Saturday afternoon, while the theatre was being prepared for the evening séance, we were entertained to a joint demonstration of clairvoyance/clairaudience by the medium Stephen Holbrook with psychic art by Sandy Ingham.

Tom and I had met and watched Stephen back in 1998 when he had done a charity evening with two of our friends,

Angela McInnes and Beryl Norris at the Guildhall in York. But of course he did not remember us, and you could see the name Tom Harrison meant nothing to him.

Sandy, in the normal waking state, cannot draw but in trance her hands are guided by Leo, a spirit artist, to produce the faces. Her husband, Mike, has devised a system to film the drawings as they develop. The images are projected on to a translucent screen so that the audience can watch the development. During a demonstration while Sandy is drawing, comments and other information are added around the picture, so it is essential that the medium looks at the screen from time to time to pick up on these. In the sketch, you will see the extras which were added to the picture she drew for me.

Having worked and watched for an hour we had a tea break and when we re-assembled, Stephen began the second session with the statement "Somebody has lost their husband to the spirit world – not long."

I answered that I had – three years ago. He didn't continue with a connection for me as he felt it was too distant. After a moment or two he spoke again "This is someone's Dad. He's not been gone long."

A lady called Margaret, whose father had died fairly recently, spoke up and by then Sandy was drawing a picture of her father. Stephen gave her a good evidential message.

Fifteen minutes later, Stephen again asked if there was someone who had lost their husband to the spirit world. –

> Stephen: "Is it their anniversary we're approaching?"
> I spoke up again "It was three days ago."
> Stephen: Your husband?
> Ann: Yes.
> Stephen: How long has he been gone, sweetheart?
> Ann: Three years.

S: It is you I want to speak to. Do you know what, I hate to say this, but he's never been as happy.

A: I know. He's told me.

S: Do you?

A: He loves it over there.

S: Thank God. Things have worked so fantastically since he passed away. *(A: Yes.)* Doors have opened, opportunities have come your way ....and you think – 'I know why that's happened because he's doing it for me.' Do you understand?

A: I do indeed.

S: Do you know what – he has just said 'Thank you for what you did for me.' He wants to let you know he knew a week before that he was going to die. You know that sounds false, but he did and he said tell her Tuesday. I don't know what day he died, what day his funeral was, but there is something to do with the Tuesday.

Tom's body *was* cremated on a Tuesday; it was also a Tuesday when Annemarie realised he wanted help with passing over but she had first been contacted the Friday before that, and here Tom confirms that he knew the week before.

S: He had had people come to visit .. Did you like his Mum?

A: I never knew his Mum, except in spirit, but she is a super person.

S: Do you know something ... His mum was a natural *(sweeping his hand across the audience – meaning as a medium)* (A: Yes) Do you know it wasn't accepted?... It wasn't common knowledge, but you know what she was a natural. And you know what? ... I'm going to tell you something, you obviously believe in the Spirit World ... and you do believe that your path with your husband had to cross for a reason. You were brought together after what you both so learned, to experience that life – the full life that you had. Do you understand?

A: I do. It was wonderful.

S: Let me tell you something else. They have just brought me a feather. Did you do something... Do you understand? (A: I do indeed.) They've just said mention the feather... There's a lot of moaning and groaning (*as the audience thought of Stewart's guide, White Feather*) so you must ....

Stephen continued with many pieces of information including reference to a Doris or Dorothy. (*I had been to visit our old neighbour called Dorothy (Dorrie), now in her nineties, just three days before and yes we had mentioned him in the conversation as Stephen said.*) He went on to tell me it wasn't the medication that kept Tom going – but spirit and although he loved the life here and was sad to leave me he didn't want anymore. (– *Tom had found the degeneration of the physical body in Parkinson's disease hard to cope with when he had always been so active*).

S: Is the 25th significant? ( A: Yes.) July? (A: No.)

S: *(he paused)* Let me move back to the lady... I spoke to a minute ago?... Why is 25th July significant to you?"

Margaret: It's my Dad's birthday.

Stephen: That's just passed away? (M: Yes.) Your Dad? Do you know that lady? (*he asked her, pointing to me.*)

M: Only from being here.

S: Well, you know what, your Dad has been getting some tips off your husband. (*again pointing to me; this brought laughter from everyone*). You know what, he's been giving him some instruction on how to communicate because your Dad was useless at communicating. (M: He was.) Useless!'

As Stephen was drawing back and finishing his connection with Tom, he looked up at the drawing Sandy had been doing and saw she was sketching a small cat, "This is a cat coming up here. Do you understand?"

A: Yes, I've just adopted one.

S: Bless you, look at it. It's only small.

A: Yes, Tomkin, he is small and perfectly black.

S: You haven't got anything with you with a love heart on it have you?     A: Yes, in my room. (*I had just bought a new diary and it has a heart on the cover. – Tom showing he was with me at Cober.*)

*Drawing done by Sandy while Stephen was speaking to me.*

As '1947' was added to the picture, he asked "And 1947 has some significance?" (*A: Very important.*) (*The very first photos were taken of materialisations in the Saturday Night Circle*) Fantastic!

RN was then added to the side of the drawing. –

S: And we've got the Royal Navy. (*A. That's my Dad*). If you get any more, you are paying again!"

My connection was the last of the afternoon, and after Stephen had thanked us and finished, I told him, and the rest of the audience, that the communicator had been Tom Harrison, and his mother, of course, was Minnie Harrison, the medium. The white feather is in front of Stewart's book and it was the last thing Tom drew, especially for the book, just a month before he died. Stephen had to admit he didn't know who Tom was. But by the time I got back to the tea room, Alf must have told him and he had bought a copy of Tom's book and the DVD, which I had been going to give him.

What wonderful entertainment for everyone there who knew so much about us and Stewart's Guide, White Feather. That very morning I had spoken to Stewart about the feather. He did not know Tom had drawn it for the fly-leaf of his book, because Tom never signed it.

I still don't recognise who is depicted in the drawing, even though I was told to look in the old photos. Tom has told me that he is now as he looked in the OLD PHOTO when he was thirty. Apart from the eyes and a wide smile, there is no real resemblance to Tom in the drawing. But then the portrait is not always of the person who has been communicating. Somebody recently said to me "Surely, you can't be sitting for a portrait at the same time as you are trying hard to get your words and ideas through someone else's mind!"

And the bits added to the drawing – The coin? When Stephen questioned what the circular symbol was, the word COIN was added and then 'WATCH FOR IT.'

The previous week in a sitting with the Hull home circle Freda, one of Stewart's main communicators had asked me about a coin. She too said I was to watch for it, and two months later, while staying with Kate over New Year, she also told me of a coin to come.

When I returned from Kate's after New Year, there was the mysterious presence of a tiny five-pence piece in my jewellery purse. I know there was not a coin in there before I went to England at Christmas, and there was no reason to have put one in while I was in UK. – So is this the one I have had to wait for? Perhaps so, as I have heard nothing more.

The initials? – All pertinent. T A stands for Tom and Ann, GH those of a friend and N for my first husband who is always around and had spoken to me at Stewart's circle the previous week. As I have said before he and Tom spend quite a bit of time together.

'Sue' – I later heard that a friend who should have been there that weekend was under great stress and it had been her birthday the week before.

An impressive and entertaining non-stop communication – a fine way to finish the afternoon and celebrate Tom's third Anniversary of moving to the spirit world.

However, we hadn't finished the connections for that weekend, as on the Tuesday following I had the opportunity to sit in Eric Cargill's home circle in York. I have known Eric and Gerald for over twenty years and of course this weekend I had had the link with Margaret, another member of their circle, when Tom had helped her father break through to communicate through Stephen. With the harmony between us, we had a good sitting and Tom took the chance of working through another medium.

He was able to speak quietly for a short time—telling me he knew I could hear him and he wanted to help with the writing. Then, telling me that Tom knew there was no 'good' evidence in what he had just said, Lucy, Eric's young guide, went on to show they knew about 'particular things'—about Tom having a leather bag for papers, with a zip, that would stick (*It still does.*)—that Tom was around when I was speaking to Roger, my brother's neighbour (*that morning*) and that Roger needs to slow down, there's 'too much in his head' (*Yes!*)—and about a 'fat' cat, telling me 'He sees Mr Tom.' (*I do see Tomkin watching something, nervously.*)

I know when Tom is helping me as the writing flows without me having to think of the words, and here again I was given some *good* snippets (*'trivia'*, some say) – particularly the bit about Roger – thus showing their continuing closeness. Thank you, everyone.

*Twenty-eight*

# A new beginning

Twenty years ago, as I write, back in April 1994, Tom and I were setting off on our first great adventure together – a speaking tour of Scotland. Just three venues this first time, in Edinburgh, Arbroath and Glasgow but the seeds were sown and our lives were changed.

Time and again, Tom said to me "It is up to you to continue the work when I'm gone." This I try to do, but we never know how the pattern of our work will develop. Like a great tapestry, new colours and themes are worked into it. Whereas until now, the books I have published have been about mediums gone by, and others' life stories, this time it is a story which has unfolded, gradually, over the last four years as Tom has explored his new world. He has reunited with his family and the Home Circle, who have been waiting for him. Now they can all, complete in their energies, work to bring knowledge to our level of existence. I won't say new knowledge – for is anything 'New'.

In Tom's new dimension, he has delighted in connecting with many old friends there and here, also some new ones, to advance their skills as well as his own. He is learning as he has told me, to work with many different energies. He still is there, as he always was, to help others. In the previous chapter, I told you how, through Stephen Holbrook, he told us he had helped a father communicate with his daughter.

For many of us, who do not understand the power of concentration needed in trying to get your thoughts through to a dense(r) level, it must be very frustrating for them, and you can imagine them saying "But why can't they hear me I'm shouting so loud?"

I think back to the story in Tom's book about Mr Matheson whose daughters ignored him when he, after he had died, went into the house. They couldn't, of course, see him, but he felt he was still very much alive. He had believed 'when you're dead, you're dead' but now he had to learn that was not so.

Tom's skill, it seems, is not only in helping departed souls communicate with those on Earth. The week before we heard about him helping Margaret's Dad, he was helping 'Eric', who had been long in the world of spirit, to speak through the human voice mechanism so that he could teach others in the spirit world how to do that.

When Katie Halliwell and I sit with Kate, we know we are in for something extra-ordinary, but this connection with spirit was something rather special and totally unexpected. It was the first time we had sat together in Katie's home near Halifax, but that didn't stop the wonderful spirit team pulling out all the stops. About half-way through the sitting we heard a chuntering lip-smacking, tutting sound and a voice shouted: "Hello, Hello!"

After I had answered "I can hear you," this amazing conversation took place.

> Voice: Yes, yes, yes. Well, this is strange indeed. I.. (*the voice almost chokes*) I .. (*quietly*) Right, right. One moment, please. (Ann: OK.) I've got to give the factor of recognition. (Ann: Yes, please.) (*In a stronger voice*) Well, on the earth plane I was Eric, in the spirit plane I am still Eric... So Eric is coming to say hello to you. I'm trying to manipulate the jaws which I haven't manipulated for a long time and I'm finding it rath..rather difficult, but bear with me, please.
>
> Ann: You are doing really very well.

Eric: Hello, hello. How do you do? Well isn't this absolutely spectacular?

A: It's wonderful, it really is.

E: Yes, Ohh .....I've just been given the opportunity to try out the mechanism and speak with you, and to pass on the grateful thanks for all the thoughts and the kind... to help me on my way. And yes, yes indeed, yes indeed and ... I've got to shove off. (Katie: Oh dear, well nice talking with you.) But I do thank you for the experience 'cos now I can take this back to my group and pass on what...

A: Would we have known you when you were here?

E: Would you indeed?

A: I've known a few Erics but...

E: Yes, but I have met with your Thomas and he's showing me the ropes, although I popped off before him.

A: Oh, did you, right. Do you remember your second name that you had here when you were on the earth?

E: Ohhhh. I need to think. I really need to think about this because names are so not important anymore. I have to think about the trousers I wore... ohh... I understand the Midlands and I'm trying to give some thoughts to the Midlands and the place where I frequented. Yes, it is quite confusing when it is the first connection.

A: It is, you have to work so hard at keeping that connection, I know.

E: And I'm aghast that there is so little that I remember, yet I can use the speaking mechanism. (A: Yes, some things are important to us and some things are not.) I remember the name Marshall if that is important – I remember the name Marshall. Hmm .. but it is so very, very different when you return to ...what you say... the vibration your earth can give and to try ... we are... Ohh! There are lots of hands steadying myself. (A: Good, you've good support.) but I have progressed enough to join a group and I have been chosen for the experimental stage so that I can report back that communication on – shall we say, different levels is possible, totally possible. So then we must give thought and practise to this so that we can gain, shall we say, the seeds of truth.

A: Yes, by gaining those seeds you gain progression too.

E: Yes, indeed, yes indeed … Ahh right, yes… I am listening to the instructions on my side of life.

A: We understand that.

E: So that I can sp.. I am quite, quite amazed that I can move the lips and move the jaw and speak. And I can hear the words that have been spoken on the earth plane that I haven't heard for a long, long time. Because the sound is not in the spirit realms as we know on the earth plane and this is what is rather marvellous. So I take this experience back with me and I can produce the experience. Do you understand what I am saying? The experience is replicated and produced just as I am speaking to you from the spirit world. I can now speak to the group and give the experience of what I and you have experienced at this time.

A: So the sound of speech you are able to pass on to your group in the spirit world?

E: And the mechanism.

A: So they learn and possibly they can come and speak.

E: And also develop this – you would say 'the mediumship' so that we have mediums. (A:Yeees??) Yes, I know it sounds complex but look at it as interesting and amazing.

A: It is fascinating.

E: It is not one way, my dears, it is two, three, four – a hundredfold ways. You are seeing but one – one dimension. When we return with the knowledge and the experience we are unfolding a hundred times, a thousand times. Shall I go on and express more? (A: I think we have got the picture.) This is why the work is vital on the earth plane, for those that return to the spirit plane with no knowledge and must begin at the very, very beginning again.

A: Right. Yes, I see what you're implying.

E: We are not all about coming and proving we are here,

we are also taking the knowledge back...

A: And that helps the people who have no knowledge.

E: You have heard of the Halls of Learning? (Katie: Yes.) This is part of the work of learning. (Katie: Right, so we are entering the Halls of Learning with you.) Is there any difference? You must open your minds because you are linked and a part of all the work – All the work.

Katie: That's interesting....

E: I have been quite the teacher. (A: You have.) I have been quite the philosopher! I have been more than Eric! (*We could hear the excitement in his voice.*)

A: You are ....Eric the Teacher.

E: I thank you for the experience, my dears, I thank you for this wonderful team that, unfortunately, your eyes cannot see, but I'm sure you feel their presence and their energy. (Katie: Yes, thank you.) This is their work so you are allowed to be a part of the work, but the larger work is being allowed for spirit to be part of the work. There are so little openings on the earth plane that we have to replicate the earth plane knowledge in the spirit plane. (A: Yes, we have a lot of teaching to do here.) We have reversed the mechanism. Good night, my dears.

A: Thank you so much for all of that.

E: My gratitude is [in] abundance with yourselves.

A: Thank you so much.

And we think that receiving messages or working as a medium is just for our benefit here in this level of existence.

Tom told me, that when they asked Aunt Agg what she did in the spirit world, she had told them she was still working as a medium to connect with those who had progressed, but wished to speak to others on the lower level.

Monsignor Hugh Benson told us how they had used ordinary speech when they first went to the spirit world until they found that all could be transmitted by thought. Recently Dr Eben Alexander also experienced this in his journey, while in a deep coma. He writes in his book *Proof of Heaven,* of the young woman who appears alongside him that: ...

> Without using any words she spoke to me. The message went through me like a wind and I instantly understood that it was true. I knew so, in the same way that I knew the world around us was real – was not some fantasy...

Now, we have 'Eric' telling us how they do need to have more people in the spirit world who can still speak, in the same way, as we do on earth. So they may help souls who are stuck in the 'physical' mode to learn and move on in spirit, because they have not learned this on earth. Now because of Tom they came to us, with Kate as our medium, to learn how to do just that and then, maybe, they will work with other trance mediums here to push our knowledge forward.

How privileged we are to be able to do this! We certainly have a lot of work to do to help people here understand the great adventure that awaits us all.

Uri Geller stated recently in *Psychic News* that he believes at some time in the future everyone will be telepathic. – But until then we think of it as a 'special' gift or just plain 'weird'. When in fact, it should be a normal practice as experienced by so-called 'primitive' people in the 'bush'. How much we have lost in our civilising processes!

However, that wasn't the end of surprises that evening for we were treated to a visit by Katie's mother. Working through Kate for the first time, and returning to her old home, she needed the help of Tom's steadying hand.

But let me give you the whole conversation and let you feel the emotion:

*We then heard a man's voice.* 'Ann, Ann.'

Ann: Come on, love, come on then, dear.

Voice–(Katie's Mum): I've been trying, been trying .. Let me touch you...

Katie (KT): Do you want me to hold your hand? (*Katie put out her hand*)

A: Has he got your hand ?     KT: Yes.

*With that a deep voice boomed* "I'm here I'm here." (*It is Tom.*)

KT: Well done, well done. Lovely to talk to you again.

Voice: Can you feel me?

KT: I can feel you. I'll tell Christine all about it. Yes I can feel you definitely. He's got his hand in mine. He went straight to it as well, no fumbling.

A: He hit my knee too.

Raven: Raven is controlling. We have two links. We have female on the right. We have male on the left. Raven try to control the vibration between both.

A: Thank you, dear Raven.

Tom: Ann, Ann, (A: Yes, yes, my dear.) I'm here. (Ann: Yes.) Here I go. What an effort it's been. Did you see my glasses? (A: I thought I did.) The dark, the dark – my glasses. Best job I could do. (A: That was a good try.) I'm linking, holding on to a beautiful lady and it's for Katie and she's wobbling about but you've got her vibration through her hand. (KT: Yes, I'm holding it now.) Wonderful, wonderful experience! (*as he says this the voice changes and becomes softer and emotional*)

KT: Yes it's fantastic.

Mum: For you, you feel, you feel it.

Tom: (*in a deep voice*) She feels. (KT: She's moving my hand.) and I am speaking for her.

KT: Yes I'm feeling it. The back of her hand. (*Mum gasps a sob.*) (*As Katie held her Mum's hand she became very cold and shivery, then very emotional. We understand that this was because the connection of the hands allowed her mother's emotion, at holding Katie's hand, to come through.*)

A: Steady, dear.

Mum: Oh my aaha....

KT: I know it's your hand.

*(Katie's Mum speaks quietly, in a light female voice but the recording is not clear enough to hear what she says.)*

KT: You did very well indeed. *(as Mum continues to sigh)* Wonderful, thank you.

Tom: Ann, I'm back!

A: You're back, switching between the two.

T: I'm back. (A: That's lovely.) What a good job's been done tonight. (A: Fantastic job, it really has.) **Rhoah!** *(a roar of triumph )*

A: *(laughing at that familiar sound)* - Yes, Darling.

Tom: God bless you, my love, got to leave. God bless, love from us all.

A: And love from us to you all.

KT: It was quite emotional.

R: Raven bids you welcome and I will bring baby bird to you. (A & KT: Thank you, Raven.) All blessings, good night. God Bless.

*We heard small sighs and were told not to be alarmed as it was the residual energy ebbing away.*

Lady's voice: Good night, my dears. (A. *recognising her –* Goodnight, Aunt Agg.) Aunt Agg blesses you and God keep you safe while on your wonderful, wonderful journey on this earth plane that we once frequented and gained so much knowledge and it is your turn to have this wonderful, wonderful chance of progression. Good night, my dears, and God Bless.


That had been an amazing and wonderful evening of connection between the two worlds. I don't know if you can appreciate the complexity of this last contact, but the team in the world of spirit had engineered it so it was possible for Katie to feel her mother's hand – and she feel Katie's, while I was able to hold Tom's hand and feel his love, just as he could feel my love for him. This is so precious for them, as well as for us, to continue to feel those beautiful vibrations which are created between us.

The 'roar' was his special way of expressing triumph at something he had achieved.

If you have understood that messages are not only comfort for us, as we grieve, but also an experiment and experience for those who contact us, then you will understand that we need to expand the knowledge here on earth of what is ahead of us and how much more effective we can be in the world by the power of thought.

So yes, we too are at a new beginning – each of us.

I am not yet at the age Tom was, when we met twenty years ago, and although I long to join him and Norman, I know how important it is that I continue here to help and encourage others. Help them know how to improve and concentrate their thoughts for knowledge and good in this world, so that many, many people may have their lives touched and we have Heaven on Earth.

As the song[1] says:

> I believe in the people of all nations
> To join and to care for love.
> I believe in a world where light will guide us
> And giving our love,
> We'll make heaven on earth.

And by this love between us, understand how we live on through all eternity.

---

1. "I Believe" was written by Pence, Jeffrey Curtis/sloan, Eliot Walker / Senatore, Matthew Joseph and has been sung by R. Watson, K. Jenkins & A. Botcelli.

*Twenty-nine*

# Life without end

When I wrote the previous chapter, I thought I had completed the book, although Tom had told me there was more to come. As he had already covered many of the different ways of communicating, I did not know what else he might do. What did happen was not something new, as you might have thought, but more of the same. However, it gave me a chance to touch many more lives.

This summer, the author whose book I was completing, asked if we might meet up while she was at the Arthur Findlay College, Stansted Hall in Essex. This was where, in 1967, Tom was given his life task, to tell people what he had experienced through his mother's mediumship and the importance of knowing that Life goes on. The result of which my life was changed – but so too were the lives of many, many others.

I checked the AFC programme and decided I could treat myself to a week there. During that week this summer I was privileged to work in a group tutored by Tony Stockwell. He really stretched our horizons and made us work. I believe that Tom thoroughly enjoyed himself too.

He connected with six of the students that week, each day presenting different aspects of himself. The only day he didn't work was Friday – his earthly birthday! Well, I suppose everyone should have a day off on their birthday, and it gave a chance for my mother and my aunt (her sister) to get a look in.

As soon as we started he was there, working with Christine Conley. She gave me a good contact but the best part, from an evidential point of view, was him talking about 'a son with him'. No, I told her, all his children are still here.

"But there is a young man with him whom he would call 'Son'." – Of course, Jonathan, his cousin's son who had passed since Tom. Tom always addressed younger men of the family and close friends, as 'Son'. Excellent proof of his survival and presence there.

One of the other memorable connections, detailing aspects of his physical life, was later on the Sunday. As recipients we had only to answer 'yes' or 'no' so the comments in italics are explanations for you, the reader.

Brenda described a man around 5'10/11" greying, thinning hair, always wore glasses. He was smart and had presence – when he entered a room everyone was aware of him – and the smile. (*Most definitely correct.*)

He looked good for his age. She felt he was showing himself between 60-70. (*When we met he was 75 but looked 60+*)

She felt there was some heart pain. (*a sudden fibrillation problem, aged 88 years, which landed him in hospital for four days – eight years ago to the day!*)

She was unable to give a definite relationship – maybe father/grandfather? (*Well, he was old enough to be my father and we used to joke about it, but he was a father of six, a grandfather – and great-grandfather.*)

He had children (Yes) and siblings. (*No, but I know where you are, I told her. – He had spent a lot of time with his future wife's family when they were growing up together, so her brothers and sisters were like siblings to him. They used to take the youngest one out for a walk in her pram.*)

His home was neat. Liked things neat. (*Definitely.*)

He was in management; he had authority. (*Yes – he was in management for a lot of his working life, – including being the first Manager at the College we were in, at Stansted Hall.*)

He wished he had achieved more of his dreams, and I must go for mine.

As she was finishing the contact she suddenly became aware that he was my husband, and the love and emotion he showed overwhelmed her. Brenda liked to work standing up and had done so today, but, at that point, she had to sit down. I shall never forget the look of surprise on her face as she felt the love. This connection was so different from the usual small pieces of evidence (trivia) but very accurate, and for her – had a surprise at the end of it.

At the coffee break on the Sunday morning, we were given the opportunity to book private sittings with the tutor-mediums. I felt I did not need a sitting and as others queued I went to get coffee for Christine (my new pal) and myself. When I got back, they were still queuing but most of the places had gone. I suddenly felt impelled, out of curiosity really, to ask about Maureen Murnan's *Medicine Wheel* sittings. All those had been taken, and just one normal sitting left. No, I didn't need one of those and I turned away, but seconds later I had to turn back and book it.

Now, in hindsight, I know why – Tom wanted to re-connect with Maureen and, through her, link to me. We had met her eighteen years before, on a very hot summer evening, when she had invited Tom to give his talk at Bourne church in Lincolnshire.

For this sitting on the Tuesday morning, Maureen and I agreed to let whatever needed to come through do so. I didn't need an evidential sitting to prove the existence of survival, or soothe my grief. I thought I knew where I was going, but I was happy to find out what the spirit folks wanted to say to me.

We had a lovely time. Maureen told me that she felt Tom there, so strongly:

> I think he is the driving force, very much behind you. I think that he has shown you over and over again that he has not left, that he's around – that he's doing things.
>
> You know you came to be a teacher. That's what you enjoy the most. That's what lights you up, when you come alive, and he'd love to be able to do that.
>
> He wants you to know the spirit world took good care of him, and when his time came, they were more than ready for him. He was able to go quite peacefully at the end, quite easily and the amount of people that were waiting – I see a line of people ready to applaud – like when someone walks into a room.
>
> He's got a wicked sense of humour, hasn't he? He's done things in the home that's made you actually stop and laugh because you've thought 'you devil I know that's you.' He draws my attention also to a white flower, and I think he is bringing it as a memory. They look like white roses. (A: *If it is white roses I know – it is the Yorkshire rose.*) It was pure white, and you know how a sheepish, shy boy would stand in the doorway if he's courting. And he's holding this white flower, and he's got a grin from one side of his face to the other (A. *That is so him!*). He's just holding it out to you, so he's obviously very proud of that emblem the Yorkshire Rose.

We are both from Yorkshire and proud to be so. A friend, who was even more enthusiastic, once bought us a flag to fly. But here in Spain we don't have anywhere to fly it, so we didn't put it up – but it was a lovely thought.

> Tom thinks he was very lucky in his lifetime 'cos he got to live his passion and travel with his passion as well.

I don't know if you have something on a computer screen that goes around and you see his face in different poses coming up. (Ann: *Yes.*) It makes you smile, and you always tell him you love him, and he loves that. He waits for that because when he knows a certain picture will come around, you'll look at him and tell him how much you love him. He just wishes he could get his voice across to say that.

And one thing I do feel he is going to experiment with if he hasn't already is EVP. I think he was interested in that (A: *I set up the Journal for Anabela Cardoso.*) Well, he's going to be trying something. He's working at this. It's my project he said that I'm working on, to get the voice across, but he wants it to be recognisable as his. 'I even want my accent because that will prove that it is definitely me!' He says that that gap is not as big as you think it is. So I think he's quite excited at that. I can imagine him being very excited at that.

He's also made a point of finding out a lot about the pioneers. He was very interested in the history; how it all started. He's made that his work as well over the other side – to find out as much as he can about them. And to meet up again for discussions with people like Gordon and Albert Best and all the old-time mediums from the very beginning.

Whenever we took the Sunday services at the centres here in Spain he would base his address on one of the pioneers.

He said out of his mother's work came a big blessing for him. She never got the accolade in her lifetime for what she did, so he made sure she got it.

I always includes 'Min' in all the talks I do on physical mediumship because Tom enthused me so much at the talk in Bourne. I always say that every time you watched him talk about it you were with him. You were part of it, 'cos you could see the man relived it all over again, and it made you live it. I remember Aunt Agg – I still listen to the recordings even now, – and that is making him smile.

He was a gentleman in every sense of the word anybody who knew him would never say anything other than that.

Towards the very end of the sitting Maureen said:

You do know that there is a little gentleman who works with you. The feel, the smell, the energy of him is very Buddhist. He's lovely, absolutely lovely and I got a glimpse of the orange robe. (*I told her of Ching Lee and how we now work together.*) Lovely, and he's got a lovely sense of humour that matches Tom's very well.

I told her that he calls Tom – 'Tom-Tom'. So here too Ching-Lee is making sure I know he is with me – one team together. As she finished the sitting Maureen told me that she had heard him also mention the name 'Sunrise'. Yes, I confirmed, that is Minnie's guide but he also had worked with Tom throughout his life and now comes to me, too.

"Ah well, you might be having more influence from Sunrise as well." she added.

As we parted and I thanked her, Maureen said "It was a privilege to be able to talk to him again."

I know too that Tom enjoyed the re-connection with a good friend.

In conversations throughout the week, I talked to a number of the students about Tom being the first Manager at the Hall and that his mother was a materialisation medium. Many people had not heard of her. Tony frequently caught me talking about the phenomena, so on the Tuesday he said "I think we will have to find a slot for you to talk about Physical Phenomena."

That slot was during the Thursday afternoon free choice time and I was allocated the Blue Room. It is not a large room and it was packed. I told them a little of Tom's experiences with the phenomena and in answers to questions I was able to tell them of my experiences of ectoplasm with Stewart Alexander. It opened quite a few eyes, and minds, to a world beyond mental mediumship.

It was a wonderful opportunity to do the work Tom wants me to do. I am most grateful to Tony for giving me a chance to do a talk, back in the place where Tom was first told to 'Get out there and tell people ...'.

It was also the place Tom gave his last talk, just four years earlier, on Eric Hatton's special annual event – the J.V. Trust week, only seven weeks before Tom quitted this physical life.

*Tom's final talk aged 92, at the J.V. Trust Week, August 2010 and the only one he has ever sat down for.*

This summer Tom has also made a new friend in Switzerland.

In July, Christine Lerch was in touch, thanking me for having the Alec Harris book translated into German and wishing to order Tom's book in English. She told me of a circle she was sitting in with friends, where they had successful table tilting. She told me "Within about one year we got some nice results, knocking, raps, fragrances. The table was several times fully levitated."

In my reply, I suggested that she invited Tom to make himself known.

In late August, this is the email I received:

> Yesterday we were sitting at a table séance with friends. The energy was very strong and the table literally galloped round the room.
>
> The table went to every sitter and we were able to ask questions. We had raps, knocks and movement of the table in the rhythm of the music. As it came to me, the movement was very gentle and I greeted him. I did as you said and I spoke direct to Tom.
>
> The reaction of the table was very violent in a positive way.
>
> I was sandwiched between chair and table. It was not possible to move the table even one centimetre, so strong was the energy.
>
> I spoke and laughed while the table hopped and pushed me without a break. As if to say: "You see, here I am."
>
> I felt a direct connection from heart to heart and was overwhelmed. Then the energy became gentle and calm. Suddenly a thought shot through my head – "Minnie is here." So I asked directly "Tom, is your mam here?" A knock on the table was the confirmation and it started to hop again. I was so touched that I then just thanked them and was simply happy in the moment of time.
>
> I did not know what I should ask, I was very touched by the happening. The energy of Tom was standing right behind me, sincere, large stature, humorous and yet very serious about the whole thing.
>
> The evening was very energetic from then [on], many knocks, full levitation of the table and lights which looked like shooting stars.

At the closing round, I thanked all spirits and especially Tom, as he was so heavily involved. I invited him to participate with us in the home circle and a knock confirmed this again. I also asked him if I can tell this experience to you, the answer came back by knocking. A very clear yes.

I felt him very close, directly behind me and was filled with happiness.

For me, it is always amazing how we are all connected. I never had in mind that an English spirit might [or] would be part of our circles here in Switzerland, but it seems like I was limited in my imagination.

It also shows me how important each one of us is and how important our actions are. Even if we do not see it at the moment or feel insignificant.

The love I could feel yesterday evening shows me how much we are guided and protected on our way, through those in spirit world.

I need to stress here that Christine did not know Tom always called his mother by the very northern English term of 'Mam', so that had been a very special close mental connection between Tom and Christine. Again, a month later, she has repeated – "What I felt and heard during the table-tilting, came from such a loving soul, it still gives me a shiver when I think of it."

Many people could tell you how special Tom's hugs were. So when someone would sneakily whisper to me that Tom was hugging another pretty woman, I always told them there were plenty of hugs to go around. To him everyone deserved a loving hug.

In October, as I was checking through all the emails and records I had kept of Tom's connections, I came across the record of a sitting with Kate back in April 2012 – two and half years ago! Kate had already told me Tom was 'dipping into clairvoyance, to kinetics, noise and wanting to be felt and don't forget aromas'. Then she talked about a group. At the time, I thought Tom might be referring to a group I already knew about, but as I read it afresh I realised that he had been forecasting the work to be done with Christine and friends as they are working with spirit on a different kind of photographic 'experience'. This is what Kate said:

> Would you understand Switzerland? There's a connection there and there will be a connection there. There's something ... He's talking about a medium connected with Switzerland would you understand. On a spirit level cos he's talking about a spirit link. He's talking about a group being formed or is being formed and again I'd like to say physical rather.
>
> He's talking about experiments, like experimental work rather than messages and there is an interest there because there's going to be information fed about the energy techniques that's been evolved upstairs.
>
> He wants to say as well that this energy, colour, form they are working with, not only comes from spirit, [but] going a little bit beyond. It's a blending of energy that they are bringing down through the layers. It's real and there is much, much work and he's quite interested in this because he likes the experimental side. Messages are fine but he likes the experiments, it excites him, it interests him.

It sounds exciting. However, these are early days in the experimentation and Tom's work will continue wherever it is needed and he feels he can make a contribution.

For forty-three years, Tom toured and talked. He spoke on radio programmes across the world – from Radio Cleveland in North Yorkshire in 1989 to Jeff Rense and Richard Syrett in North America in 2004 and Barry Eaton in Australia in 2005. He appeared in TV programmes and videos, including his own, made with the help of friends. All this he did to let people know that Life is eternal and we live on, as spirit, after so called 'death'. More important to him than the fact we survive was the knowledge that we can communicate with each other across this divide.

As we are able to instantly talk and write to each other across our globe so can we with all those who have made the great journey into what so many call 'the unknown'.

It is not totally 'unknown' and our knowledge of it grows, constantly. Some of the wonderful direct voice recordings through Leslie Flint, (and reported in Neville Randall's book), give us insights into some travellers' worlds. As do the books of Anthony Borgia. No doubt, as aspects of our world have changed since those times, forty – sixty years ago, so might there be changes in aspects of the spirit world.

Tom has not told me a great deal about the world he is in, except that it is 'BEAUTIFUL!' – far more beautiful than he could have imagined. The family are all together. He had forgotten how they looked, but they are as in the old photo. (see the group photo opposite) as he is too – looking as he did around thirty-years-old – in his prime – which is why Gilly didn't instantly recognise him when he returned to her after just one week in spirit.

He has also said he is amazed how much they have progressed in their knowledge of the Truth and now he is having to catch up.

Through Kate, I know that he is still talking to groups. Telling them what life is like on earth now. Though the mind boggles as to how he describes computers and being able to send emails across the world each morning! We also know now he is helping others learn how to communicate with the physical level.

As he is always so busy working, I sent out the thought as to what he did in his spare time. The answer came back, again through Kate, to whom he showed himself playing Bowls! – which he loved.

I do know he has our cottage ready for us and, thanks to Lynne, that there is a wisteria in our garden, with beautiful blue hanging flowers, which he sits under. (Here in Spain, to my great sadness, mine refuses to flower!)

*The Saturday Night Club Circle - 1948.*
*Left to right, top row: Mr Jones;, Tom; Tosher, his father; Sydney*
*Seated: Mrs Hildred; Minnie, Tom's mother; Doris, Tom's wife;*
*In front: Gladys Shipman, Syd's wife.*

I am also told that my first husband, Norman, talks to people, especially those who are still stuck in their old beliefs and 'churchianity'. He is helping them to expand their views, to be able to move on, to grow and progress in the knowledge and application of Natural Law.

To those who worry about what happens when you have been married more than once. I still don't know how it will work. I have had two wonderfully happy, loving marriages. I love them both dearly, and to know that my two husbands get on well together in spirit, and there are 'no problems' between them, then may be − hopefully − we will all be together, to travel on in love, when I get over there to join them!

This is what David Fontana wrote on the subject, in his book *Life Beyond Death* (2009):

> ... communicators insist that the emotion of love survives death, and that lovers are reunited and continue their loving relationships. However, Christ informed his listeners that the resurrected 'neither marry nor are given in marriage' (Luke 20:35). Marriage, as a legal bond, seems to belong to this world only. In the afterlife individuals are drawn together solely through love, and it may be that a man or a woman can love − and be loved by − several people at the same time, with all concerned untroubled by possessiveness or jealousy.
>
> The bonds of love between people are therefore much closer and function at a much deeper and less selfish level. Close relationships formed on earth can be renewed and deepened, while new relationships with those of like mind can be formed. If ultimate reality really is love, as the great spiritual traditions assure us, we can assume that at each successive level of the afterlife individuals draw closer and closer together until the bond of love is fully realized.

*Thirty*

# A desire to communicate

Throughout these chapters has been one theme – the desire of one man to show that what he had said was true – communication is possible – and in many ways. He liked to use an old saying, at times attributed to Professor Charles Richet and at others to Sir William Crookes, but which ever said it, it is applicable to all their research into the Afterlife:

"I did not say it was possible: I said it occurred."

Because Tom believed so strongly in proving survival and communication between the worlds, he made it his business to connect with as many people as he could in that first year. I calculate that he worked with fifteen different mental mediums, where the message was directed to me, and five others where the message had been for someone else and I was told of it later. He supported his friend Eric, who saw him when in need of healing. He spoke through three trance mediums, two of them he used several times. He materialised twice, once in Spain and once in UK. And he materialised again briefly through another medium, in Spain, in his second year.

He has been seen more than once through transfiguration with two mediums, and in the second year, during a séance with more than thirty people, he spoke via an independent voice box; also that afternoon, writing a message for me on a sheet of paper .

He has worked with several people in the early stages of mediumship development; through a professional 'stage' medium – non-stop for over twenty minutes and through a good friend, in an impromptu sitting, passing on very good information for over an hour. Then this summer he added another eight new connections to his list!

When medium/psychic artist Sandy Ingham stayed with me, Tom did not come through to have a concentrated session with me, but popped occasional comments into her mind – as a host would do to a guest in his own home, and as always his lovely (sometimes wicked) humour came through.

He has worked hard, developing his skill with many different energies and abilities; making himself seen, heard and felt by the mental mediums. He has learned to manipulate a voice box, move various objects (and tables) and control the weight of ectoplasm. With these skills, he is helping others in the world of spirit to improve their communication ability, as we heard through Stephen Holbrook and Kate Maesen.

Tom and the Saturday Night Club Circle are working now with other earthly circles so that this wonderful connection between the two worlds may grow, to help others understand the importance of this knowledge.

The knowledge that we live on, and how we live here, and what we do matters – here, and maybe for eternity or until we can remedy the errors we make.

This is not the end of the story for it will go on eternally, but here is where I will close for now.

May you find your direction;
   make your own connections;
      develop the 'Desire to Communicate'
         and may the blessings of all life go with you.

Synchronicity

The moments when worlds collide
Seemingly at Random
As our thoughts, our actions are mirrored
by an unknown intrusion
from somewhere beyond
and in that second, the meeting
takes on a special significance.
A memory is ignited and love lit.
Which came first the distant act or ours?
Who can say –
But the action of the collision implies
harmony
a reassurance that what we do
is met with approval.
We are where we should be –

And "all's well with the world".

*Ann Harrison - March 2013*

# Time-line of Tom's communications and my experiences from October 2010 to September 2014.

This is to give you an idea of the continuity of the communication.

## Key to abbreviations:

| App. | Object brought from another place | phen | phenomena with possible classificat'n |
|---|---|---|---|
| CA | Clairaudience (mental hearing) | Phenom | Phenomena not poss to classify |
| CS | Clairsentience (mental feeling) | Phys | Physical phenomena |
| CV | Clairvoyance (mental seeing) | Spt Wrt | Spirit writing (no human contact) |
| CC | Cross-correspondence | Telep | Telepathy: phys to spt /spt to phys |
| DRV | Direct Radio Voice | Tf | Transfiguration (face changes) |
| DV | Direct voice away from medium | Tk | Telekinesis (movement of objects) |
| Mat | Materialisation | Tr | Trance |
| Men | Mental mediumship (inc CA, CS, CV) | TV | Trumpet voice |

| Date | Type of contact | Medium | Detail |
|---|---|---|---|
| **Oct** | **2010** | | |
| 15-23 | Men | Annemarie | Worked with Tom pre passing. He was 'Just waiting'. |
| 24 | Men | Pat F. | Rob recog. description of Tom + Agnes 'popped in'. |
| 30 | Men | Gilly W. | 13 good correct facts. Felt pre-passing condition. |
| 30 | Men | Belinda G. | Saw him with Gilly as she worked. 'Likes flowers.' |
| 30 | TV/Phys | Stewart A. | Sunrise spoke to me through Trumpet in séance. |
| 31 | | Steve B. | Nr Trance. AwareTom taking power for me to speak. |
| **Nov** | | | |
| 5 | Men | Kate Circle | Sitters heard 'Tom' called. Kate saw him smiling. |
| 6 | Tr | Steve B. | Tom spoke for 5 mins with help from Guide. |
| 9 | Men | Micky B. | Vision of Tom, 10 good facts. Tie shown & received. |
| 16 | Tr | Stewart. A | Home Circle. Tom speaks well. Chris verifies voice. |
| 17 | CA phen | AH | A strong Spanish 'Ole' as I woke. |
| 18 | CS/Telep | AH | Felt Tom's pain in head; then sensed 'Potatoes'. |
| 21 | Men | Morag B. | May Anniv. - too many tears. T. sits in special chair. |
| 25 | Men | Eric B. | Sees & hears Tom after reciting T's favourite joke. |
| 26 | CA phen. | AH | Metal pipe being struck to ring, at Tom's side of bed. |
| 26 | Men | Ray B. | Tom visited Ray one morning. A Surprise but happy. |
| **Dec** | | | |
| 1 | CA phen. | AH | Beep-beep of child's horn. Felt Tom cuddled in beside me. |
| 10 | CA phen. | AH | Waking, heard Tom's voice say - 'plastic roller blind'. |
| 12 | Men | Gay N. | At Acacia Centre told Rob 'Thomas will always be here.' |

| Date | Type | Medium | Detail |
|------|------|--------|--------|
| 13 | CA phen. | AH | 4pm, sound of spoon on cup but spoon on worktop. |
| 13 | Phenom | AH | Bright flash of light end of lounge -EH Book completed. |
| 23 | CA phen. | AH | Waking - sound of drink's can 'popping'. |
| 25 | CA phen. | AH | Waking - heard Tom say 'Cheese' as for photo. |
| 25 | Tk phen. | | Lounge Lamp base switch moved, not usually used. |
| 31 | Phenom | AH | Woken by a kiss. Saw Tom in favourite M&S shirt. |
| **Jan** | **2011** | | |
| 3 | CA phen. | AH | 'Bonngg' of mattress spring moving from across the bed. |
| 28 | Tr/Tf | Kate/Circle | Aware of Tom. Sitters saw his wide smile - transfiguration. |
| 30 | Men | Morag B. | Good connection. Flowers for B/day ( Norman's 4 days ago). |
| **Feb** | | | |
| 18 | CA phen. | AH | 7.15 Ping-ping /crack /CLUNK to get me up for garage trip. |
| 21 | CA phen. | AH | 7.15 Honk-honk of rubber bulb type horn. |
| end | Tr | Gilly W. | On trance course, Tom spoke through her re trumpets. |
| end | Men | Chris M. | Waking vision of Tom & book - 'Will see you in séance.' |
| **Mar** | | | |
| 6 | CA phen. | AH | Tom says 'It's now time' (to get up to collect Kate). |
| 6 | Men | Kate M. | Felt his head pain. Lot of good evidence given. |
| 9 | Men | Kate M. | Tells me Tom will hold my hand. |
| 10 | Tr | Stewart A | Tom says 'a bit of a struggle is an understatement.' |
| 13i | Telep | AH | During service thought 'Take them to Mar Menor.' |
| 13ii | ? | AH | Redirected along road to take them to Mar Menor. |
| mid | Men | Raglan Circ | Sitter heard name 'Tom' called. They felt him there. |
| end | DRV | Anabela | Had recording of Tom saying 'Sou o Tom'. |
| **Apr** | | | |
| 1 | Tr / Phys | Kate M. | Long talk with Tom, felt energy, saw his hands transform K's. |
| 8 | Tr | Stewart A | Tom laughs & comments on tree planting, previous day. |
| 12 | Men | Alf W. | Sees Tom doing healing for me. Logo on pullover. |
| 25 | CA phen. | AH | 7.15 Grating clink of lid being put on Wedgewood box. |
| **May** | | | |
| early | Men | Doreen C. | Tom tells her they are doing all they can for her. |
| 12 | Telep | AH | I send out thought 'What's the temperature like?' |
| 17i | M | Barbara Mc | Hears Tom say 'No more long trousers.' |
| 17ii | Tr | Rob McL | Tom speaks for 3 minutes - confirms he's in shorts. |
| 26 | Tr | Stewart A. | T. tells guest sitters I'm 'sunning myself' (Ibiza). |
| 27 | Tr / Phys | Kate | Sunrise speaks. Sitters see orange feather in K's hand. |
| **Jun** | | | |
| 12 | Telep | AH | Sent out thought 'Did you really do DRV?' |
| 14 | Telep | AH | Was turned off my motorway in Leeds to visit Eric! |

| Date | Type | Medium | Detail |
|------|------|--------|--------|
| 16 | Tr | Stewart A. | Tom says Jackie safe. Re DRV - 'You know the answer.' |
| 21 | Men | Barbara Mc | RE DRV : Tom says he can do more than boil an egg now! |
| 30 | Tr | Stewart A. | Tom says feels he has run 10 miles (effort to commun.) |
| **Jul** | | | |
| 3 | Tr | Frederick S | Portugal, Tom spoke briefly, greets us, no record kept . |
| 9 | Men | AH | Telling Julie Tom gives pain in my head - he modified it! |
| 14 | Tr | Stewart A. | Tom - 'Love to all' & 'tell them -They ain't seen nothing yet.' |
| 15 | Tr/Men | Kate M. | Sunrise & Tom spoke. K said someone playing fiddle. |
| 20 | Telep | AH | Impressed to read Lyceum Manual, solved Kitson puzzle. |
| 21 | Tr | Gilly W. | Sunrise likes new trumpet, give strength for her to work. |
| 21 | Men | Julie G. | Tom took over email. T.Likes how I stood up for myself. |
| 22 | Tr/Tf | Kate M. | Tom's eyes seen clearly. Forgotten how 'heavy' earth is. |
| 22 | Men/ CC | Gilly W. | Tom 'Ann, new book in her head' & ref to a wheelbarrow. |
| 25 | Telep | AH | I sent out thought what to call book about Tom. |
| 25 | Telep | AH | 'Only connect, only connect' running through my head. |
| 26 | Tr | Rob McL | Sylvia told us 'Tom present with Barbie and SB.' |
| 28 | Men | Kate M. | Saw a figure build. Heard Tom say Harrison Connections. |
| **Aug** | | | |
| 5 | | AH | I write to Kate M. 'Communications a good title.' |
| 6i | Men | Kate M. | In circle, Tom says got his wings, K saw RAF roundels. |
| 6ii | | cont. | Plus - Ann has moved rug and he moved a spoon. |
| 7 | Men | Kate M. | Tom corrects email, saying 'NO! Connections!' |
| 9 | CA phen. | AH | Woken by 3 raps on SOLID wooden door. |
| 10 | Tk/CC | Violet E | Table sitting. Tom flying table and connecting. |
| 11 | | | A Phone call from Violet re table. I emailed Kate. |
| 12 | Men/ CC | Kate M. | In circle Kate heard 'Table tilting, Lifting table.' |
| 13 | CC | | Kate emailed me re hearing Table tilting - WOW! |
| 22 | **Mat** | David T | Tom materialised, kissed my forehead, spoke some time. |
| 22 | **Mat** | David T | Tom then spoke to Robin & Rob. Sunrise materialised. |
| 25 | Men | Chris M. | Good evidence from Tom in public Dem - laughter. |
| **Sep** | | | |
| 7 | Tk | | Small swan and glass block moved in Sanctuary display. |
| 7 | Men/ CC | Kate M. | Hears Tom's accent. People singing about wheelbarrow. |
| 15 | **Mat** | Stewart A. | Tom ruffled my hair, held my hand but lost control of form. |
| | **Mat** | Stewart A. | He re-mingled and spoke. Yes to Q re swan move. |
| 30 | Tr/Men | Kate M. | While in trance, Tom 'took' K to meet his Mam & A. Agg. |
| **Oct** | | | |
| 14 | Men/Phy | Kate M. | Felt Tom so close she 'became' him, younger but same. |
| 14 | Men | Jo (K's daug) | 'Saw' A. Agg - spoke about material - robes? (Jo's work) |

| Date | Type | Medium | Detail |
|------|------|--------|--------|
| 16 | Men | David D. | Tom gave Vera Lynn, 'We'll meet again'. He's with Derek. |
| 23 | Men | Rob Mcl | Tom tells me not to work so hard & take my vitamins. |
| 30 | Men | u/k | At Cober told of 3 messages to others through year. |
| 30 | Men | workshop | Evidence from Tom via Violet, Paul, Yvonne & 2 others. |
| 30 | Telep | Carol | Gave toast of 'Happy Days'. |
| 31 | Telep | AH | Felt impelled to suggest Martine to be sitter at Kate's. |
| **Nov** | | | |
| 11 | Tr | David F-R | Keep bed clear you will feel him. He likes you to wear cross. |
| 12 | Tr/ Phys | Scott M. | Daniel, Scott's helper passed on evidence from Tom. |
| 12 | Telep | Barbara Mc | Got out 8 sets of cutlery & plates for 7 of us. No Tom! |
| 12 | Men | Scott M. | Found Tom easy to connect with mentally. |
| 14 | Men | AH | Clearly heard Tom say 'Are you ready for breakfast?' |
| 14 | Men | Annemarie | Felt need to send cat card to Kate - Good link. |
| 15 | CA phen. | AH | Clearly heard Ding-ding to wake me to get jobs done! |
| 20 | CA phen. | AH | 7.15 'Raspberry' behind my head and a 'Ding'! |
| 23 | CA phen. | AH | 7.15 Sound of piece of wood being dropped. |
| 25 | M/Phys | AH | In TV Prog *Heartbeat* felt my hand being held - icy cold. |
| 26 | CA phen. | AH | Three separate taps and another click in bedroom. |
| 26 | Phenom | AH | As I woke, I felt his kiss - amazing feeling. |
| **Dec** | | | |
| 4 | Tk | AH | The pillow was out of bed in the morning. |
| 5 | Men | Darren B. | Fred G. told a 'Harrison connected with Bertha Harris'. (Yes) |
| 8 | Men | Barbara Mc | Felt acute indigestion - puff pastry - aware of Tom. |
| 20 | Phenom | AH | Felt hair being gently ruffled (top left, new sign of Tom). |
| 22 | Tr | Rob Mc. | Tom spoke - 'leaving table to the experts'. All felt him there. |
| 24 | Men | Kate M. | A.Agg - Love to all. Tom on rounds. Ann'll feel him. |
| 25 | Phenom | AH | Felt presence (heat) snuggling against me as he would. |
| 26 | Phenom | AH | Felt hair being played with as I sat quietly after lunch. |
| 27 | CA phen. | AH | 7.30 Strong clunks from bedroom furniture. |
| 28 | Phenom | AH | Felt hair played with while working late on ITC Journal. |
| **Jan** | **2012** | | |
| 10 | Phenom | AH | As I voiced a good idea, I saw a man-sized flash of light. |
| 26 | CA phen. | AH | Sound of bedside cabinet being dragged then dropped. |
| 29 | CA | AH | Various voices while I was ill (Flu?). Felt healing sent. |
| 29 | CA phen. | AH | 'Tap on b/side table. I said 'Hello Love', louder tap in reply. |
| 29 | Phenom | AH | Felt Tom close - hair was ruffled. |
| 31 | Men | Barbara Mc | Saw Tom with photo frame. Said he'd moved it. (Yes) |
| **Feb** | | | |
| 5 | Men | Rob Mc. | Good mess. for Joyce. Tu'penny rice/Tom will move table. |

| Date | Type | Medium | Detail |
|------|------|--------|--------|
| 7 | **Mat** | Kai M. | Tom materialised in séance , touched my knees. |
| 10 | Tk | group of 4 | Table movement started when we sang 'Tu'penny rice'. |
| 15 | Tk | AH | Nutmeg grater moved to worktop while at the freezer. |
| 16 | Tk | circle | Table confirmed Tom had moved grater. |
| **Mar** | | | |
| 2 | Men | Eric B. | In vision he 'saw' Tom and Jackie in market. |
| **Apr** | | | |
| 4 | Tr/ Phys | Stewart A. | I held Tom's hand while he spoke through S's trance. |
| 12 i | Men | Kate M. | Tom tells of Swiss connection to come & experiments. |
| 12 ii | Men | Kate M. | He's into clairvoyance, kinetics, noises - he wants to be felt. |
| 19 | Men | Kate M. | Portugal - do more writing. Explains lifetime link with Kate. |
| 22 | CS phen. | AH | Could smell perfume. K has said this would happen. |
| 26 | Men | Lynne J. | Tom told L. of his painting & gave 'Yellow & blue'. |
| 28 | CA/CS | AH | Woken by Tom's 'pleasure' sound as he snuggled in. Felt it |
| 29 | Men | Scott McL. | Accurate evidence Scott could not know about Tom. |
| **May** | | | |
| 16 | Men | Ray B. | Tom visiting him regularly. |
| 29 | Tr | Rob Mc. | Tom spoke. Watching me, knows what it is like. |
| 30 | Men | Kate M. | Tom passed many details on what I had been doing. |
| 31 | Tk | Circle | Crazy Table. Tom pushed it into me - pneumatic drill sound. |
| **Jun** | | | |
| 3 | Men | Rob Mc | Two Tom's present. Lot more to come for book. |
| 7 | Tk | Circle | Table pushed at me. Tom been to see Maggie re tree. |
| 16 | Men | Ray B. | 1 Hour sitting. Susan working with Tom. Lots good evidence. |
| **Jul** | | | |
| 19 | Tk | Circle | Table - sounds of saw & hammering - me mending broom. |
| **Aug** | | | |
| 23 | Tk /Men | B. Mc/Circle | Aware of WW1 soldier. Table confirmed as Willie Earle. |
| 30 | Tk | Circle | Table with me /dancing - re Street Party? I agree to go. |
| **Sept** | | | |
| 19 | DV/ Phys | Scott M. | Tom spoke via voice box. Also wrote a message. |
| 24 | Men | Kate M. | Tom has met the Wimbledon folk (Bob & Ena Brake) |
| 26 | Tr | Kate M. | Ching Lee spoke to say we are all 3 working together. |
| 30 | Men | Rob Mc. | Aware of Tom standing back to let Aunt Agg speak to me. |
| **Oct** | | | |
| mid | Tk | AH | Remote control for Hifi unit went missing. |
| 30 | M/Phys | Peter E. | In séance , knew Tom was near / Trumpet sign of $\infty$ |
| **Nov** | | | |
| 22 | Men | Paul H.(Class) | Spiritual man - wore socks with sandals; waved his stick. |

| Date | Type | Medium | Detail |
|------|------|--------|--------|
| 25 Dec | Men | Paul H ( serv) | Aware of Tom - talking about a light left on all night. |
| 13 | Men | PaulH(class) | Shown a cauldron. Tom 'Bells are ringing' (booked Xmas). |
| 13 | Men | Lynne(class) | Vision of Tom in Halls of Learning - re-learning all he knew. |
| 17 | Men | Barbara Mc | Tom says my Xmas tree is different this year. |
| 18 | Men | Barbara Mc | Tom - 'We wrote letters to each other. ' ( I read 2 days ago) |
| Feb | 2013 | | |
| 5 | CS? phen. | AH | Woken with feet being firmly held. |
| 5 | Men | Kate M. | Tom told her of my new friend (cat?). In his shorts - my |
| | | cont/d | Spanish weather has been warm enough for shorts. |
| 14 | Men | Carol (class) | Saw a bright twinkly eye - As I saw Tom's every day for drops. |
| 14 | Men | Paul ( class) | Had I lost a remote control? (Found it last week) |
| Apr | | | |
| 13 | Telep | AH | Gilly reminded of wheelbarrow. I saw vision of shed on it. |
| 19 | Tr/ Phys | Kate/Circle | Tom tries building, walks 3 steps (not seen but we felt him). |
| 21 | Tr/ Phys | Kate/KT/AH | Tom speaks late - bring trumpet in, write in his notebook. |
| May | | | |
| 20 | Tr/ Tf | Rob McL. | Trance dem. Tom seen, greets students, spoke to Lynne. |
| 29 | CA phen. | AH | Sounds 'Ping, dragging cupboard, footsteps (slippers). |
| Jun | | | |
| 16 | CA/CS | AH | Heard 'Like a cup of tea?' Felt a tingle like an electric shock. |
| Jul | | | |
| 15 | CV/ Psy | Circle in Port | Two of the students connected well with Tom. |
| 17 | Tele/ M | AH / B McL. | Tom -Slow down or you'll be having a near miss. (take time) |
| 17 | Tr | Kate M. | Tom controlled her, during phone call to speak direct to me. |
| Aug | | | |
| 5 | CA phen. | AH | Strong knock on cabinet, I said I heard it, so another knock. |
| 7 | App/ Tk | AH | My mislaid fan appears in my guest room. Not there before. |
| Oct | | | |
| 17 | Tr/ Phys | Stewart A. | Took Eric to circle. He spoke to Jackie. I spoke to Tom. |
| 19 | Men | Kate M. | Tom gave her Piaf, 'Je ne regrete rien' - He never did. |
| 20i | Tr | Kate M. | Spt Eric told us Tom had helped him communicate. |
| 20ii | Tr /Phys | Kate M. | Tom helps Katie's mum come through. Both speak. |
| 27 | M/Tr | Steven H. | Excellent evidence in public dem + Sandy's drawing. |
| 30 | Tr | Eric C. | Tom to help me with writing. Zip sticks on his doc. bag. |
| Dec | | | |
| 10 | CA phen. | AH | 7.15 Sound of cup put on to wooden surface. |
| 12 | CA phen. | AH | Loud knocking on glass door - no one there. |
| 13 | CA phen. | AH | 7am Man's voice said 'Bu-Bub' (my cat's pet name) . |

| Date | Type | Medium | Detail |
|------|------|--------|--------|
| 31 | Men | Kate M. | 11.45pm Tom came in with Susan. Been to S.Af.- H.N.Year. |
| Jan | 2014 | | |
| 16 | Men | Lynne J. | Tom sitting under Wisteria in flower. 'Hello Love', smiling. |
| 23 | Men | Carol B-M | Acorn. London conn. Good character description of Tom. |
| Feb | | | |
| 2 | Men/CA | Rob | Tom says special anniversary (Syd died 10yrs today, but it is also Rob & Barbara' McL's 10th anniversary.) |
| Mar | | | |
| 14 | Men | Carol B-M | 'How do I begin' - wanted to finish song & hug & kiss me -Tom |
| Aug | | | |
| 3 | Men | Christine C. | Cheesy smile, warm handshake, notes in book. 'Son'. |
| 3 | Men | Angie | Disciplined man, good snippets of him. |
| 3 | Men | Brenda | In management, liked authority. Felt his love for me. |
| 4 | Men | Rosemary | Good: His age, war experience, good with men, pacifist. |
| 5 | Men | Maureen M. | Very good close connection. Plenty of evidence & advice. |
| 6 | Men | Carol | Felt his love for his wife, loved visits to me, wrote a book. |
| 7 | Men | Audrey | Felt his closeness briefly as we had other work to do. |
| 9 | Phenom | | Airport "Always look on the bright side" song played in shop. A |
| | | cont'd. | strong memory of Tom's last visit to Stansted Hall. |
| 22 | Tk /Men | Christine L. | Table circle in Switzerland. Tom makes himself known. 'Hugs' |
| Sep | | | |
| 11 | Tk | AH | Peeler appeared on worktop while I was looking for it. |
| 11 | Men | Barbara Mc. | Tom showed her an English breakfast. (I buy it for M&J today) |

Many of the incidents and connections included in this timeline are not detailed in the chapters throughout the book but nevertheless they happened and you can see from the range that Tom has been very busy and has a strong 'desire to communicate', no doubt roping in all who would teach and help him.

The connections have not stopped, but four years is the limit I have put on them as I finish this book.

So I leave you now with Tom's most favoured way of closing his talks:

He who knows not and knows not that he knows not,
is a child – teach him.

He who knows not and knows that he knows not,
is a fool – shun him.

He who knows and knows not that he knows,
is asleep – waken him.

But he who knows and knows that he knows,
is a wise man – follow him!

*Attributed to Omar Khayam,*
*13th-century philosopher*

*Tom showing interested listeners some of the artifacts from*
*the Saturday Night Club circle, after one of his talks.(2009)*

# What do we mean by...[1]

**Apport** – an object brought from another place without physical contact, usually into a closed room during a séance. It could be from another room or from a distance and be of any size depending on the energy available from the medium or the circle members. (eg. flowers, coins, badges watches, etc.)

**Automatic-writing** – The mind of the spirit writer acts through the sub-consciousness of the writer (automatist). The hand of the medium writes without knowing what is being written. This is sometimes so definitive that foreign languages, and the signatures of deceased persons have been written. Paintings, drawings, and maps are also produced. By this method the underground foundations of the original Glastonbury Abbey were revealed to Mr Bligh Bond, the architect. His excavations afterwards proved the statements and maps to be true.

**Banners** – I suppose these could be likened to those banners carried by organisation like the British Legion and Irish organisations at the head of their parades, and described in the *Lyceum Manual* by the visionary Andrew Jackson Davis in 1863 as follows – "Each group was headed with a banner of a given colour, and each child belonging to that group wore a badge or sash of the same colour as that of their banner." Davis learned that there is a language of colours which is studied and taught in the Summer-land; and each group wore the colour that symbolised its degree of spiritual unfoldment.

1. Many of these explanations are from the *Spiritualists' Lyceum Officers' Manual* (1957).

**Cabinet** – a small enclosed space which the medium sits in, usually of cloth or wood, used in materialisation and direct voice séances to condense the energy required for physical communication by the spirit people.

**Clairaudience** – or clear hearing is hearing sounds and voices not registered by the physical ear. The faculty by which mediums obtain audible messages from spirit people. The speakers may also be seen clairvoyantly. The names, dates, and other information received establishes the identities of the communicators.

**Clairsentience** – feeling emotion and/or physical attributes of the deceased person. It may even be a form of impressionism in which the medium appears to be changed into another person. The medium then speaks and acts like a deceased friend, who may be recognised by the characteristics exhibited. (see also Overshadowing)

**Clairvoyance** – or clear seeing is seeing pictures or people not by the use of the physical eye. The faculty by which sensitives/mediums describe distant places, or peoples, or see the forms of deceased friends and relatives, and describe their characteristics so minutely, that their personal friends are able to recognise them immediately. Other mediums read sealed letters, and give appropriate replies.

**Circle** – a group (usually a regular group) of people sitting together for development of spirit communication.

**Direct Voice** – (sometimes known as Independent Direct Voice) the voice of the spirit person speaks from somewhere in the room, away from the medium, by the use of a structure known as a Voice Box. Leslie Flint was a foremost exponent of this method of communication. He was seldom in trance (as is usual) and would often join in the conversation with the spirit people.

**Ectoplasm** – A term coined by Charles Richet around 1894 to mean exterialised-substance. A substance taken from the body of a suitable medium which can be manipulated by the spirit chemists into any material form they wish – skin, hair, beards, clothes – fabric, soft or coarse.

**EVP** – Electronic Voice Phenomenon where voices unheard by the human ear at the time of recording are impressed on to magnetic tape in a tape recorder using a background of 'white noise' or natural sounds.

**DRV** – Direct Radio Voice. Disembodied voices from the deceased heard through a radio tuned away an unintelligible station, very often a language not understood by the listener, and very different from the language received.

**Healing** – Everyone who is sympathetic automatically projects a healing force towards the sufferers. Others, by prayer and co-operation with spirit friends, often obtain marvellous results. Disorders that have been given up by doctors as hopelessly incurable are sometimes cured. Trained healers usually direct the flow of power through their hands to the seat of trouble sensing where they need to work without being told by the patient.

**Instrumental Transcommunication** – The use of TV, phones, radios, tape and digital recorders by the spirit people to communicate with us in pictures and sound.

**Kinesiology (applied)** – is a technique in complementary medicine claimed to be able to diagnose illness or choose treatment by testing muscles for strength and weakness. One branch comes under 'Touch for Health' which is a system of balancing the body posture, attitude and life energy to relieve stress, aches and pains, feel and function better, be more effective, clarify and achieve your goals and enjoy your life!

**Lyceum** – The Spiritualists' Sunday School teaching the Spiritualist way of life. First formulated on earth by A. J. Davis in 1863 from visions he had had of teachings in the spirit world.

**Materialise /materialisation** – A physical manifestation of a spirit person. Parts of the body, or hands and faces are built up and seen in dim light or against a luminous plaque. At other times the entire human form is visible and tangible, and often speaks. It can, with permission, be touched and feels solid and human like. This is usually in red light.

**Medium** – a person through whose organic structure departed spirits can communicate with people in this life.

**Mental mediumship** – this includes clairvoyance, which does not use the physical eye; clairaudience, which hears sounds and voices not registered by the ear; clairsentience (see above) and telepathy, in which the whole consciousness of man operates miles away from his physical body. *(See Chapter 18 The Clairs- communication through the mind)*

**Noah's Ark Society** – named after researcher/supporter Noah Zerdin who worked a lot with the development of Leslie Flint the Direct Voice Medium.

**Overshadowing** – a spirit may blend their personality with the medium's aura so the medium takes on the characteristics of the spirit person. They then transfer their thoughts to the medium, who may speak those thoughts directly without actually going into a trance state. (see also Trance-light.)

**Phenomenon/a** – an occurrence/s, the cause of which raises a question. In Spiritualist terms something (usually physical) which happens through the action of spirit influence on our physical world.

**Psychic faculties** – also called intuition - phases of consciousness possessed by all mankind. Derived from the

Greek word 'psyche' meaning 'soul'. (includes the 'clairs') A **Psychic** does not necessarily connect with departed spirits.

**Séance** – a group of people meeting and sitting together, often in the dark, in an attempt make contact with spirits of the 'dead' and to witness the physical phenomena produced by the presence of spirit people (spirits of the 'dead').

**Silva Mind Control** – The Silva Method teaches students specialized guided imagery techniques to rewire their subconscious and negative programing, enabling them to tap into their true potential and achieve their goals. José Silva developed 'Mind Control' to help his children do better in school and increase their chances of success in life. Since then, this dynamic meditation technique has evolved into a sophisticated mental training program that is offered in seminars in over 129 countries around the world.

(A) **Sitting** – see séance. Also applied to an appointment with a psychic to obtain information, such as divination /fortune telling/card readings etc, or with a medium for contact with spirit family and friends.

**Spirit Writing** – Writing carried out without human contact with the pen. Usually done in the dark. The result may or may not be in the style of the spirit while here on earth. (*see Ch.23 Eastbourne, September 2012.*)

**Table communication** – a method used by the early pioneers to communicate with the spirits. This is done by placing the hands of the sitters *lightly* on the top of the table and allowing it to move by their combined psychic energy. Communication can be by spelling out the alphabet until the table responds or by asking carefully worded questions to receive replies. We used one movement for 'Yes' and stillness for 'No' – minimum effort (energy) used.

**Telepathy** – the consciousness of man operating possibly miles away from his physical body to transmit ideas and thoughts to someone else. There are many recorded events of its use by primitive peoples. It also applies to spirit friends who deliberately transfer thoughts to us for our guidance.

**Trance (light)** and inspirational speaking – these are mental states in which the medium's spirit self is influenced, so that his normal powers are greatly expanded.

**Trance (the deep state)** – the person may appear to be asleep/unconscious and may be insensitive to pain. In this state it easier for the spirit people to speak directly through the medium even producing their own accents. In exceptional circumstances, entirely new ideas are expressed, even foreign languages, which the medium has not learned, have been spoken.

**Transfiguration** – This results from the energies around the sensitive's head becoming illuminated and changed in form. Sometimes, an ectoplasmic formation alters the shape and size of medium's features so that a spirit person may be recognised. The two phases do not often occur together. It is sometimes due to a spirit strongly overshadowing the medium. Occasionally this may only be seen clairvoyantly but is frequently seen with the physical eyes

**Trumpet** – a conical megaphone to amplify spirit voices, usually being moved near to the recipient by spirit means. It requires a great deal of concentrated effort to make a voice physically heard in our world so a megaphone is used.

**Voice box** – a structure developed by the spirit scientists to enable a spirit voice to be heard away from the medium. Usually constructed of ectoplasm extracted from the medium's body. Tom told me when they were shown it in their circle, it resembled a rose with moving petals.

# Bibliography

Here is a list of the books used or referred to in this book:

Alexander, Dr E. *Proof of Heaven*, (2012): Simon & Schuster NY; also available as an e-book

Alexander, S. *An Extraordinary Journey*, (2010): Saturday Night Press Publications (SNPP) UK.

Borgia, A. *Facts*, (1946 & New Ed 1995): Two Worlds Publishing Co. London.

Borgia, A. *Life in the World Unseen*, (1945, Rev. 1995): Two Worlds Publishing Co. London.

Brake, G & R, *Of Love between Two Worlds*, (2011): Saturday Night Press Publications (SNPP) UK.

Butler, T.&L. *There is no Death: There are no Dead.* (2004): AA-EVP Publications, USA.

Cardoso, A. *Electronic voices: Contact with another dimension?* (2010): O Books, London. (The CD is available from www.itcjournal.org)

Dixon-Smith R. *New Light on Survival*, (1953): Rider & Co, London.

Findlay, J. A. *On the Edge of the Etheric*, (1931) (many reprints) SNU Publications.

Fontana D. *Life Beyond Death*, (2009): Watkins Publishing, London.

Forster E.M. *Howards End*, (1910): many reprints.

Halliwell, K. *Eperiences of Trance, Physical Mediumship and Associated Phenomena with the Stewart Alexander Circle (Pt3)*, 2011: Saturday Night Press Publications (SNPP) UK.

Harris, Louie. *Alec Harris: The full story of his remarkable phyical mediumship*, 2009: Saturday Night Press Publications (SNPP) UK.

Harrison, T. *Visits by our friends from the other side.* (1989 & 2011): Saturday Night Press Publications (SNPP) UK.

The DVD *Visitors from the other side* and the *Minnie Harrison ChristmasParty CD* are available from: www.snppbooks.com .

Harrison, T. *Life After Death: Living Proof,* (2008): Saturday Night Press Publications (SNPP) UK.

Keen, M. Ellison, A. & Fontana, D. *SPRs Proceedings on The Scole Report,* (2011): Saturday Night Press Publications, UK.

Lodge, Sir O. J. *The Reality of a Spiritual World,* (1930): Ed.Benn, London.

*Lyceum Manual,* (1924 edit): British Spiritualists Lyceum Union, UK.

Northage, I. & Marshall, B. *While I remember: the Life story of Ivy Northage,* (1998): Coll.of Psychic Studies, London.

Parker, D & J. *Atlas of the Supernatural,* (1990): Prentice Hall Press, N.York.

Randall, N. *Life After Death* (1975) R.Hale & 1987 Corgi Edit, London. Repub by R. Hale (2001) on amazon.com.

Swaffer, H. *My Greatest Story,* (1945): Allen & Co, London.

Swaffer, H. *My Talks with the Dead,* (1945): (extracts from *My Greatest Story*) Spiritualist Press, London.

Thomas, Rev C.D. *Life Beyond Death with Evidence,* (1928 reprint 2006): Hesperides (see amazon.com) or download M.Tymn's excerpts at www.aeces.info/Legacy-Section/Bios-)

Tymn, M. *Difficulties in Spirit Communication Explained by Dr James Hyslop* (see www.provingparanormal.com to download pdf.)

Walsch, N.D. *Conversations with God: book 1,* (1995): Hodder & Stoughton, London.

All Saturday Night Press Publications books are available from our website www.snppbooks.com or through amazon sites.